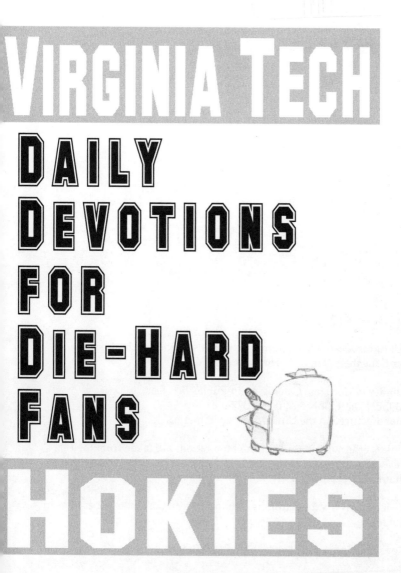

VIRGINIA TECH

DAILY
DEVOTIONS
FOR
DIE-HARD
FANS

HOKIES

Daily Devotions for Die-Hard Fans: Virginia Tech Hokies
© 2011 Ed McMinn

All rights reserved, including the right to reproduce this book or portions thereof in any form whatsoever.

Library of Congress Cataloging-in-Publication Data
13 ISBN Digit ISBN: 978-0-9846377-0-6
Manufactured in the United States of America.

Unless otherwise noted, scripture quotations are taken from the *Holy Bible, New International Version*. Copyright © 1973, 1978, 1984, by the International Bible Society. All rights reserved.

Visit http://www.die-hardfans.com for information about other titles in the series.

Cover and interior design by Slynn McMinn

Every effort has been made to identify copyright holders. Any omissions are wholly unintentional. Extra Point Publishers should be notified in writing immediately for full acknowledgement in future editions.

HOKIES

To the Stansfields,
Scott and Mikara,
their daughter Natasha,
and especially their Hokie son, Jason

IN THE BEGINNING

Read Genesis 1, 2:1-3.

"God saw all that he had made, and it was very good" (v. 1:31).

The school was called VAMC for short, their colors were black and gray, and their first game was against a private boys prep school. But they were the beginning of Virginia Tech football.

Back in 1891, the school that was to become Virginia Tech was known as Virginia Agricultural and Mechanical College. A few of the cadets would gather in the afternoons to play some rugby, and the games caught the attention of school president John McBryde, who authorized the organization of an athletic association and the launching of a rudimentary football program.

Professor Ellison A. Smyth served as the first coach and team manager. He joined with student W.E. Anderson, who was Virginia Tech's first-ever football captain, to assemble a team.

On Oct. 21, 1892, football officially began at Virginia Tech with a game against St. Albans, a private boys preparatory school in Radford. Of this primitive game, it was said that "whoever found himself holding the ball ran with it and prayed not to lose any teeth." Despite playing right tackle, Anderson scored the first touchdown in school history as VAMC won 14-10. St. Albans won a rematch eight days later 10-0 in a game that was shortened by a disagreement over the rules.

Team members purchased their own equipment, including the

football, which cost $1.25. Overall, enthusiasm among the student body was not exactly at a fever pitch as the players frequently had to scour the barracks to find enough warm bodies to practice.

Smith rolled his charges out of bed at 6 a.m. and sent them off on a cross-country run before breakfast. The team practiced in a wheat field, the boundaries laid off by a plow. An early yearbook said the field "was about as level as a side of Brush Mountain."

It was, though, a beginning.

Beginnings are important, but what we make of them is even more important. Consider, for example, how far the Virginia Tech football program has come since that first practice field was laid out with a plow. Every morning, you get a gift from God: a new beginning. God hands to you as an expression of divine love a new day full of promise and the chance to right the wrongs in your life. You can use the day to pay a debt, start a new relationship, replace a burned-out light bulb, tell your family you love them, chase a dream, solve a nagging problem . . . or not.

God simply provides the gift. How you use it is up to you. People often talk wistfully about starting over or making a new beginning. God gives you the chance with the dawning of every new day. You have the chance today to make things right – and that includes your relationship with God.

They had to use lots of persuasion to keep two teams on the field, for everybody wanted to play on the first team or none.
-- The Bugle *on the scarcity of football players in the early going*

Every day is not just a dawn;
it is a precious chance to start over or begin anew.

MIRACLE PLAY

Read Matthew 12:38-42.

"He answered, 'A wicked and adulterous generation asks for a miraculous sign!'" (v. 39)

Some disappointed Tech fans were already filing toward the Lane Stadium exits when the Hokies pulled off a miracle.

On Sept. 19, 2009, the Hokies were down 15-10 to Nebraska. Tech had the ball but also had 88 yards of real estate to cross and only 1:44 in which to do it with an offense that had managed a grand total of 55 yards in the last half. Fat chance -- and some exiting fans certainly thought so. Not Frank Beamer. There's "always a chance when you have Tyrod," he said later. Tyrod was quarterback Tyrod Taylor, who led the Hokies to "one of the most miraculous finishes in Beamer's 23 years as Tech coach."

From the 12, Taylor dropped back to pass and was immediately pressured. Wide receiver Danny Coale saw that his quarterback was in trouble and turned upfield. Taylor spotted him and let fly. "I just kept running as fast as I could," Coale said, "and I looked up and saw the ball heading right into my hands." "I just wanted to give him a ball he could catch," Taylor said later.

He did and Coale did. As those exiting Tech fans stopped in mid-stride and watched in wonder, Coale raced all the way to the Husker 3 before a shoestring tackle got him down. Coale thought he had scored, but an official review marked him out of bounds. The play had covered 81 yards.

But the miracle wasn't over because the Cornhusker defense that had stymied the Hokies the whole half wasn't about to quit. Taylor was sacked on first down at the 11 and forced to throw the ball into the band on second down. But then on third down with 33 seconds left, Taylor rolled left, couldn't find anybody open, came right, and fired a bullet to flanker Dyrell Roberts. He was covered but he made the catch. Touchdown. 16-15 Tech. Miracle.

Miracles -- like last-minute scores to pull off a comeback -- defy rational explanation. Escaping with minor abrasions from an accident that totals your car, for example. Or recovering from an illness that seemed terminal. Underlying the notion of miracles is the idea that they are rare instances of direct divine intervention that reveal God.

But life shows us quite the contrary, that miracles are anything but rare. Since God made the world and everything in it, everything around you is miraculous. Even you are a miracle. Your life thus can be mundane, dull, and ordinary, or it can be spent in a glorious attitude of childlike wonder and awe. It depends on whether or not you see the world through the eyes of faith. Only through faith can you discern the hand of God in any event; only through faith can you see the miraculous and thus see God.

Jesus knew that miracles don't produce faith, but rather faith produces miracles.

Oh, my goodness gracious!
— *Defensive coordinator Bud Foster on the miraculous finish*

**Miracles are all around us,
but it takes the eyes of faith to see them.**

DAY 3

IN A WORD

Read Matthew 12:33-37.

"For out of the overflow of the heart the mouth speaks. The good man brings good things out of the good stored up in him, and the evil man brings evil things out of the evil stored up in him" (vv. 34b-35).

Eleven-point underdogs against Virginia, the Hokies looked like it the first half, being thoroughly dominated. And then head coach Bill Dooley had a few choice words to say at halftime.

In 1985, Tech limped into Charlottesville with a 2-4 record that included losses to Cincinnati and Richmond. The Hoos weren't much better at 3-2, but they were solid favorites. They proceeded to virtually blow Tech out of the stadium in the first half, outgaining the Hokies 241-49. They led only 10-0, though, which left Tech very much in the game.

Defensive back Carter Wiley, who lettered for four years and was selected by the Atlanta Falcons in the 1988 draft, recalled what happened at halftime in the Tech locker room. Since Wiley persistently had a problem with the heat, he was "sitting in the corner, soaking in ice, and listening to Dooley." What the coach did was attempt to fire up his players by challenging them personally. Said Wiley, Dooley was "walking up to every one of us and saying, 'Is this the way you play football? Is this the way you want to be remembered? Is this who you are?'"

Wiley cautioned that "There was not anything devious or

ill-directed" about the coach's approach or his words. "Dooley always just tried to get each one of us to come together to make something happen."

Whether it was Dooley's words or something else, something did happen for the Hokies. Behind alternating tailbacks Maurice Williams and Eddie Hunter, Tech rushed for more than 200 yards the last half, scored on its first four possessions, and won 28-10.

These days, everybody's got something to say and likely as not a place to say it. Talk radio, 24-hour sports and news TV channels, late-night talk shows. Talk has really become cheap.

But as Coach Bill Dooley illustrated, words still have power, and that includes not just those of the talking heads, hucksters, and pundits on television, but ours also. Our words are perhaps the most powerful force we possess for good or for bad. The words we speak can belittle, wound, humiliate, and destroy. They can also inspire, heal, protect, and create. Our words both shape and define us. They also reveal to the world the depth of our faith.

We should never make the mistake of underestimating the power of the spoken word. After all, speaking the Word was the only means Jesus had to get his message across – and look what he managed to do.

We must always watch what we say, because others sure will.

Coach Dooley raised our ire enough to go out and make a run of it again in the second half.
– Carter Wiley on his head coach's halftime words against UVa

Choose your words carefully; they are the most powerful force you have for good or for bad.

CONQUERORS

Read John 16:19-33.

"In this world you will have trouble. But take heart! I have overcome the world" (v. 33b).

J.J. Larson overcame the obstacles common to all collegiate athletes: pulled muscles, sprains, burnout, and the like. But she also battled one obstacle that made her unique among collegiate tennis players: She had only one hand.

Larson played tennis for the Hokies from 2004-08. She finished her career with 70 wins, which placed her eighth on the school's all-time win list. She was ranked No. 1 in the East at 12-under and No. 1 nationally in 14-under. All this is fairly typical for a tennis phenom.

But Larson's story was never really typical because she was born with a left arm that stops just below the elbow. She began wearing a prosthetic arm when she was only three months old. When she was growing up, the monkey bars were off limits, but otherwise she was like every other kid. Once, her father found a friend of his daughter's crying because she wanted a prosthetic arm so she could be like J.J.

Thus, Larson grew up under conditions that she described as "normal." When she was nine, her dad put a tennis racket in her right hand and told her to start swinging. She quickly fell in love with the sport and figured out how to serve by putting the ball between the thumb and forefinger of her prosthesis and

tossing it. The perfected technique became a vicious weapon as she developed a serve clocked at almost 100 miles per hour. She came up with a backhand by resting her racket on the prosthetic arm, then whipping it off with her right hand -- all of which just seems perfectly normal to the indomitable J.J. Larson.

We each have a choice to make about how we live. We can merely survive or we can overcome as J.J. Larson has done.

We often hear inspiring stories of people who triumph by overcoming especially daunting obstacles. The barriers they face may be physical or mental disabilities or great personal tragedies or injustice. When we hear of them, we may well respond with a little prayer of thanksgiving that life has been kinder to us.

But all people of faith, no matter how drastic the obstacles they face, must ultimately overcome the same opponent: the Satan-infested world. Some do have it tougher than others, but we all must fight daily to remain confident and optimistic.

To survive from day to day is to give up by surrendering our trust in God's involvement in our daily life. To overcome, however, is to stand up to the world and fight its temptations that would erode the armor of our faith in Jesus Christ.

Today is a day to overcome by remaining faithful. The very hosts of Heaven wait to hail the conquering hero.

She never uses her arm as an excuse out there. She's just a really positive influence on her teammates and her coaching staff.
-- Tech tennis coach Terry Ann Zawacki-Woods on J.J. Larson

**Life's difficulties provide us a chance
to experience the true joy of victory in Jesus.**

DAY 5

FIREPROOF

Read Malachi 3:1-5.

"Who can stand when he appears? For he will be like a refiner's sire or a launderer's soap. He will sit as a refiner and purifier of silver" (vv. 2, 3a).

James Madison?!?

On Sept. 11, 2010, the Hokies lost to James Madison 21-16 at home, one of the most inexplicable defeats in modern Tech history. The team was 0-2, and the season was in shambles. Yet, they recovered to win their next eleven games and the ACC championship. Where did they find such remarkable tenacity and determination? They followed the example of their head coach, who early in his life was quite literally tested by fire.

When Frank Beamer was 7, his brother, Barnett, and he accidentally knocked over a jug of gasoline that made contact with a fire they had built to burn trash. The liquid flames hit young Frank on his face and his right shoulder and arm, and he spent the next three years undergoing painful skin grafts, more than thirty operations in all. "I'd go in [to the hospital] for a week and have an operation and then I'd go home for a week, then come back the following week and have another operation," Frank recalled.

Beamer admitted he felt sorry for himself at times lying in the hospital while the other kids were out playing ball. But his mother would get him up and walk him down the hall. "Sure enough, in five minutes, I saw 10 people who had it worse than me," he said.

He would think, "I don't have it so bad after all."

Sister Billie said her younger brother "probably shouldn't have lived through that, as badly as he was burned." But Frank Beamer not only lived, he recovered; he persevered and triumphed, tested by fire to serve as the example for his teams when their character is likewise tested as it was early in 2010.

The vast majority of us never face the horror and agony of literal fire such as Frank Beamer did. For most of us, fire conjures up images of romantic evenings before a fireplace, fond memories of hot dogs, marshmallows, and ghost stories around a campfire, or rib eyes sizzling on a grill. Fire is an absolutely necessary tool.

Yet we appreciate that fire has the capacity to destroy. The Bible reflects fire's dual nature, using it to describe almighty God himself and as a metaphor for both punishment and purification. God appeared to Moses in a burning bush and led the wandering Israelites by night as a pillar of fire. Malachi describes Jesus as a purifying and refining fire.

But the Bible, too, uses fire to symbolize the destructive force of God's wrath, a side to God we prefer not to dwell on. Our sin and disobedience, though, not only break God's heart but anger him.

Thus, fire in the Bible is basically a symbol for God's holiness. Whether that holiness destroys us or purifies us is the choice we make in our response to Jesus. We are, all of us, tested by fire.

It was a hard time for all of us, but we made it.
-- Frank Beamer's sister, Betty, on the years of his recovery

The holy fire of God is either the total destroyer
or the ultimate purifier;
we are fireproof only in Jesus.

RUN FOR IT

Read John 20:1-10.

"Peter and the other disciple started for the tomb. Both were running, but the other disciple outran Peter and reached the tomb first" (vv. 3-4).

Though he realized he'd "never run more than 100 yards in [his] life," Virginia Tech quarterback Tom Stafford once determined to run from campus to Roanoke to win $40.

As a junior in 1965, Stafford was behind starter Bobby Owens, and he saw very little action. (See Devotion No. 70.) As a result, he spent a lot of time on the bench in the company of his teammates. One afternoon during a game, conversation got around to running long distances, and eventually someone came up with the idea of running all the way to Roanoke, a distance of a good 25 miles or so. One of the players put a pool together, securing a dollar per man, and the pot climbed up to $40.

That was a lot of money to Stafford, so he decided to make the run. One of his teammates and he set out, running "through Dixie Caverns and up and down the hills and everything" in this day before Interstate 81. His running partner quit after about an hour, but Stafford jogged on.

Several of his friends, including offensive lineman Milt Miller, escorted Stafford on the highway with a car, but finally went on ahead to Salem, "watched a movie at the theater . . ., had dinner at some hamburger joint, came back, and found me still on the road."

At that point, his teammates stretched a piece of twine across the highway close to Salem and used it as a finish line.

Even after he spent a couple of hours in the shower trying to recover from his five-hour run, Stafford could barely move the next day at practice. When coach Jerry Claiborne asked him what was wrong, Stafford replied, "Milt Miller stepped on me." Stafford waited until his senior season to tell Claiborne the truth, and the coach "got a kick out of it."

Hit the ground running -- every morning that's what you do as you leave the house and re-enter the rat race. You run errands; you run though a presentation; you give someone a run for his money; you always want to be in the running and never run-of-the-mill.

You're always running toward something, such as your goals, or away from something, such as your past. Many of us spend much of our lives foolhardily attempting to run away from God, the purposes he has for us, and the blessings he is waiting to give us.

No matter how hard or how far you run, though, you can never outrun yourself or God. God keeps pace with you, calling you in the short run to take care of the long run by falling to your knees and running for your life -- to Jesus -- just as Peter and the other disciple ran that first Easter morning.

On your knees, you run all the way to glory.

I still have that finish line to this day.
-- Tom Stafford on a souvenir of his run to Salem

You can run to eternity by going to your knees.

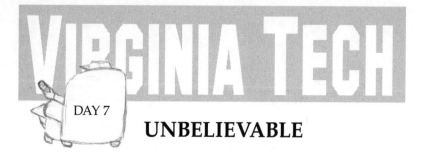

DAY 7

UNBELIEVABLE

Read Revelation 21:1-8.

"But the cowardly, the unbelieving, the vile . . . the idolaters and all liars -- their place will be in the fiery lake of burning sulfur. This is the second death" (v. 8).

What the Hokies baseball team did to the team ranked number one in the nation was simply unbelievable.

In April 2010, the Hokies took on top-ranked Virginia in Charlottesville in a three-game series. The Tech team wasn't exactly a bunch of slouches; at 25-11 the Hokies were ranked No. 20.

But the Cavs won the first two games 4-2 and 8-2, and on Sunday, April 18, they appeared to have the series sweep and their twelfth straight win over Tech at home wrapped up. They led 5-3 heading into the top of the ninth and had the nation's top closer on the mound. He proceeded to strike out the first batter. Then, however, something unbelievable happened.

The closer who led the country in saves walked three straight batters and was yanked. The new pitcher apparently had bailed the Cavs out when he struck out the next batter and then got two strikes on senior outfielder Sean Ryan. Coach Pete Hughes called time out and walked over to his batter. He told him to relax, but he was really stalling to slow down the Cav pitcher's momentum.

On a 3-2 count, Ryan walked, cutting the Virginia lead to 5-4. That brought sophomore left fielder Buddy Sosnoskie to the plate. He drilled a double off the left-field fence, clearing the bases and

propelling Tech into a 7-5 lead. Steve Domecus then added some insurance with a single that scored Sosnoskie.

When Virginia didn't score in the bottom of the ninth, the Hokies had an 8-5 win after being down to their last strike against the country's top-ranked team, leaving the home crowd sitting in silent disbelief.

What we claim not to believe in reveals much about us. UFOs. Global warming. Sasquatch. Aluminum baseball bats and the designated hitter.

Most of what passes for our unbelief has little effect on our lives. Does it matter much that we don't believe a Ginsu knife can stay sharp after repeatedly slicing through tin cans? Or that any other team besides Virginia Tech is worth pulling for?

That's not the case, however, when Jesus and God are part of the mix. Quite unbelievably, we often hear people blithely assert they don't believe in God. Or brazenly declare they believe in God but don't believe Jesus was anything but a good man.

At this point, unbelief becomes dangerous because God doesn't fool around with scoffers. He locks them out of the Promised Land, which isn't a country in the Middle East but Heaven itself.

Given that scenario, it's downright unbelievable that anyone would not believe.

Football is an incredible game. Sometimes it's so incredible, it's unbelievable.
-- *Tom Landry*

Perhaps nothing is as unbelievable as that some people insist on not believing in God or his son.

JUGGERNAUT

Read Revelation 20.

"Fire came down from heaven and devoured them. And the devil, who deceived them, was thrown into the lake of burning sulfur, where the beast and the false prophet had been thrown" (vv. 9b-10a).

The Syracuse Orangemen ran right smack into the greatest juggernaut Virginia Tech had ever put on the football field. The result was described as an "unbelievably decisive spanking" of the three-time Big East champions.

The 5-0 Hokies were ranked No. 4 in the nation on Oct. 16, 1999, when they "welcomed" 16th-ranked Syracuse to Lane Stadium. They weren't feeling much respect, however, as critics denigrated their schedule, which included wins over James Madison, Alabama-Birmingham, and a bad Rutgers team. Nobody was harping, though, after Tech slaughtered Syracuse 62-0, the largest shutout defeat of a ranked team in college football history.

"I think we made a strong statement here," said All-American defensive end Corey Moore. "We don't care what people say about our schedule." As writer Randy King put it, "This barbecue was cooked and done by halftime." Tech led 31-0 at the half after the defense held the Orange to 34 yards on 24 plays. The defense even got the slaughter under way by scoring the first touchdown. Cornerback Anthony Midget caused a fumble, and rover Cory Bird snatched it in mid-air and jogged 26 yards for the score.

After that, it was tailback Shyrone Stith from one yard out, Michael Vick to wide receiver Ricky Hall on an 8-yard TD toss -- and the carnage had begun. Tech led 48-0 after three quarters and added a couple of gifts in the fourth quarter: Defensive back Phillip Summers had a 43-yard interception return and linebacker Tee Butler recovered a dropped punt snap in the end zone.

"I believe this is a special night in Blacksburg," said coach Frank Beamer. It was the night the Hokie juggernaut got loose.

Maybe your experience with a juggernaut involved a game against a team full of major college prospects, a league tennis match against a former college player, or your presentation for the project you knew didn't stand a chance. Whatever it was, you've been slam-dunked before.

Being part of a juggernaut is certainly more fun than being in the way of one. Just ask Tech's opponents in 1999. Or consider the forces of evil aligned against God. At least the teams that took the field against the Holies in 1999 had some hope, however slim, that they might win. No such hope exists for those who oppose God.

That's because their fate is already spelled out in detail. It's in the book; we all know how the story ends. God's enemies may talk big and bluster now, but they will be trounced in the most decisive defeat of all time.

You sure want to be on the winning side in that one.

Wouldn't you be embarrassed? Of course it's embarrassing.
    -- Syracuse offensive tackle Mark Baniewicz after the 62-0 defeat

**The most lopsided victory in all of history is a
sure thing: God's ultimate triumph over evil.**

LESSON LEARNED

Read Psalm 143.

"Teach me to do your will, for you are my God" (v. 10).

Mickey Fitzgerald learned his lesson well when he was growing up. The result has been a life rich with doing for others.

Fitzgerald played for Virginia Tech from 1976-79. He has been called "one of the most versatile and talented players to ever sign with the Hokies." He started at tight end as a freshman and later played fullback, defensive tackle, linebacker, and guard. Fitzgerald was so valuable to the Hokie football program that when head coach Jimmy Sharpe was fired after the 1977 season, the school president visited Fitzgerald and asked him not to transfer to Alabama, telling him, "If you leave, whatever we've done to build this program crumbles, and it would set us back light-years."

Fitzgerald's success on the gridiron and later in life came despite deafness in his right ear and limited hearing in his left. Football was also a way out of what seemed like a hopeless childhood. He grew up in abject poverty; at one time, his family was homeless, and his brother and he were placed in an orphanage. "That was really a devastating time for us," Fitzgerald said, "but it was also, unwittingly, the best thing that ever happened to us." That's because the orphanage gave Fitzgerald and his brother structure -- and a chance to learn some valuable lessons.

Fitzgerald learned an indelible lesson from Father Paul, a priest who often took the Fitzgerald boys to ball games and other places.

One day Fitzgerald asked the priest, "Why do you do all these things for us? There's nothing we can do for you." Father Paul answered, "Oh, there's something you can do for me. One day, you'll do it for someone else."

Fitzgerald learned that lesson so well that *Virginia Tech Magazine* once said he "has made a habit of giving all he's got." He sponsors an orphanage in Atlanta and has established Mickey's Rascals, a foundation to help underprivileged children in rural areas.

Learning about anything in life requires a combination of education and experience. Education is the accumulation of facts that we call knowledge; experience is the acquisition of wisdom and discernment, which add purpose and understanding to our knowledge.

The most difficult way to learn is trial and error: dive in blindly and mess up. The best way to learn is through example coupled with a set of instructions: Someone goes ahead to show you the way and writes down all the information you need to follow.

In teaching us the way to live godly lives, God chose the latter method. He set down in his book the habits, actions, and attitudes that make for a way of life in accordance with his wishes. He also sent us Jesus to explain and to illustrate.

God teaches us not just how to exist but how to live. We just need to be attentive students.

It's what you learn after you know it all that counts.
— John Wooden

To learn from Jesus is to learn what life is all about and how God means for us to live it.

DREAM WORLD

Read Joshua 3.

"All Israel passed by until the whole nation had completed the crossing on dry ground" (v. 17b).

Peculiar as it may sound, a broken foot allowed Carlos Dixon to achieve the biggest dream of his life.

A North Carolina native, Dixon dreamed of playing basketball in the ACC. He was pretty good in high school, but not a single ACC school came calling. Virginia Tech showed the most interest. It wasn't the ACC -- it was the Big East -- but it was a major conference and big-time basketball.

A 6-7 forward, Dixon was a starter in Blacksburg the first time he put on a uniform in the fall of 2000. For three seasons, he was good but his teams weren't, never qualifying for the Big East Tournament when all they had to do was avoid finishing last.

And then before his senior season of 2003-04, Dixon's basketball world turned upside down. He suffered a broken bone in his left foot during the off-season that required surgery. His head coach was fired, replaced by Seth Greenberg. Finally, Tech was accepted into the ACC beginning with the 2004-05 season. That latter news changed everything as Dixon had already been considering sitting out a season to allow his foot to heal completely. Now by doing so, his longtime dream of playing in the ACC would come true. "It was tough watching the guys play the year I had to sit out," Dixon said, "but I knew it would all work out in the end."

It did indeed. The Hokies stunned the stuffy, proud ACC in 2004-05 by going 8-8 in the conference. Perhaps the highlight of the season came in a stunning 67-65 win over Duke. In the most important game of Dixon's life, Greenberg said his senior "was just terrific on both ends" of the court.

Playing in the ACC was Carlos Dixon's lifelong dream, and of all things, a broken foot helped make it come true.

No matter how tightly or doggedly we cling to our dreams, devotion to them won't make them a reality. Moreover, the cold truth is that all too often dreams don't come true even when we put forth a mighty effort. The realization of dreams generally results from a head-on collision of persistence, timing, and luck.

But what if our dreams don't come true because they're not the same dreams God has for us? That is, they're not good enough and in many cases, they're not big enough.

God calls us to great achievements because God's dreams for us are greater than our dreams for ourselves. Could the Israelites, wallowing in the misery of slavery, even dream of a land of their own? Could they imagine actually going to such a place?

The fulfillment of such great dreams occurs only when our dreams and God's will for our lives are the same. Our dreams should be worthy of our best – and worthy of God's involvement in making them come true.

That was his dream; he always wanted to play in the ACC.
-- Seth Greenberg on Carlos Dixon

**If our dreams are to come true, they must be
worthy of God's involvement in them.**

OF GENTLE MEN

Read John 2:13-22.

"He made a whip out of cords, and drove all from the temple area . . .; he scattered the coins of the money changers and overturned their tables" (v. 15).

Frank Beamer has been called "the consummate southern gentleman off the field." This holds true even when he suffers a reporter's little prank in the wake of a tough loss.

In 2001, the 6-0 Hokies were upset by Syracuse 22-14 at home. The loss was galling enough for Beamer, but he was particularly riled because he felt the Orangemen received a rather strange -- and illegal -- advantage in the game. It was a Dum-Dum.

After the game, Beamer complained that the Syracuse kicker had taken a butterscotch Dum-Dum onto the field to help line up his kick. Beamer compared it to an old golf trick and declared the use of the little sucker in that instance to be illegal.

The Tuesday after the game, writer Randy King stopped by a local convenience store and bought a Charm's Super Blow Pop. He then tiptoed into Beamer's office and set the lollipop in the coach's chair. When Beamer arrived, he pulled out his chair, saw the lollipop, and stared silently at it for a few moments. Then he broke into laughter and pointed at King. "If you turned that thing around and put it on the ground," he said, "and you're trying to hit that golf ball straight. . . ." Typical of the southern gentleman, the prank elicited not an angry explosion but a good laugh shared

with someone who, like Beamer, appreciated both the seriousness of and the humor in the situation.

Later that day, someone asked Tech's kicker, Carter Warley, if a Dum-Dum would help him line up a kick. "I don't see where a lollipop would help me," he said. "I would need a big old road sign pointing toward the goal posts that said, 'THIS way.'"

A calm, caring manner and a soft voice are often mistaken for weakness, and gentle men are frequently misunderstood by those who fail to appreciate their inner strength. But Frank Beamer's legendary coaching career and Jesus' rampage through the Jerusalem temple illustrate the perils of underestimating a determined gentleman.

A gentleman treats other people kindly, respectfully, and justly, and conducts himself ethically in all situations. A gentleman doesn't lack resolve or backbone. Instead, he determines to live in a way that is exceedingly difficult in our selfish, me-first society; he lives the lifestyle God desires for us all.

Included in that mode of living is the understanding that the best way to have a request honored is to make it civilly, with a smile. God works that way too. He could bully you and boss you around; you couldn't stop him. But instead, he gently requests your attention and politely waits for the courtesy of a reply.

The stuff that worries many coaches doesn't bother [Frank] Beamer.
-- Sportswriter Mike Harris

God is a gentleman, soliciting your attention
politely and then patiently waiting for you
to give him the courtesy of a reply.

VIRGINIA TECH

ONE TOUGH COOKIE

Read 2 Corinthians 11:21b-29.

"Besides everything else, I face daily the pressure of my concern for all the churches" (v. 28).

Virginia Tech has had more than its share of tough football players, but they all have to stand in line behind Greg Nosal. He is the only one tough enough to lose a section of a body part during a game -- and still keep playing.

Nosal, the starting left guard, said that as quarterback Tyrod Taylor started scrambling during the first half of the 45-21 win over Central Michigan on Oct. 9, 2010, he "went to crack back on the defensive end." During the play, Nosal's left pinkie got caught in the other player's facemask. "I just felt like it was a really bad cut," Nosal said.

Nosal engaged in a little self-treatment, squeezing his hand between plays to apply some pressure to the wound until he realized his glove was covered in blood. When the offensive series was over, he trotted to the sidelines, took his glove off, and "I see my bone sticking out." He hurried over to trainer Mike Goforth, who took one look and escorted Nosal into the locker room.

It wasn't "a really bad cut." In fact, Nosal had lost a half inch of the end of the finger. According to Goforth, "The tip of his finger was exposed, leaving just the nail and bone there." Time out was called while a search was conducted on the field for the missing portion of Nosal's finger. It was finally located in Nosal's glove.

HOKIES

Team surgeon Marc Seigel said the severed portion could be reattached and gave Nosal a choice: Do it now or put the tip on ice, keep playing, and do the surgery after the game. Nosal opted to play, went back in, and played on into the fourth quarter, coming out only when Tech had a secure 31-7 lead and thereby securing his place among Tech's legendary tough guys.

You don't have to be a Virginia Tech offensive lineman to be tough. In America today, toughness isn't restricted to physical accomplishments and brute strength. Going to work every morning even when you feel bad, sticking by your rules for your children in a society that ridicules parental authority, making hard decisions about your aging parents' care often over their objections — you've got to be tough every day just to live honorably, decently, and justly.

Living faithfully requires toughness, too, though in America chances are you won't be imprisoned, stoned, or flogged this week for your faith as Paul was. Still, contemporary society exerts subtle, psychological, daily pressures on you to turn your back on your faith and your values. Popular culture promotes promiscuity, atheism, and gutter language; your children's schools have kicked God out; the corporate culture advocates amorality before the shrine of the almighty dollar.

You have to hang tough to keep the faith.

I guess it's a big deal if your pinkie got ripped off.
— Greg Nosal on the attention his injury received

**Life demands more than mere physical toughness;
you must be spiritually tough too.**

CHEAP TRICKS

Read Acts 19:11-20.

"The evil spirit answered them, 'Jesus I know, and I know about Paul, but who are you?'" (v. 15)

It was the most successful trick play ever pulled off that none of the Hokie coaches called.

On Sept. 29, 2001, eighth-ranked Tech found itself knee-deep in a battle with Central Florida, a 25-point underdog. Early in the third quarter, the Hokies held onto a precious 19-14 lead and lined up to punt the ball away. Or at least that's what the Tech coaches -- and the players -- thought.

To everyone's surprise, punter Vinnie Burns took the snap and uncorked a "wobbly, rainbow pass" that "settled in the nervous hands of Garnell Wilds." Wilds than rambled 33 yards to the UCF 23. Six plays later, tailback Keith Burnell scored from the 2 to up the lead to twelve. The Hokies never looked back in a 46-14 romp.

Tech had worked on a fake-punt pass for fifteen minutes or so during the walk-through the day before the game. Head coach Frank Beamer said, though, that the fake was not called when the punt team lined up on fourth-and-eight at the Hokies 44.

"We did it on the run," agreed Wilds, a redshirt sophomore. "Man, I'm glad it worked out." So was Burns, a redshirt freshman who had never thrown a pass from punt formation before. "I was looking around and Garnell was wide open," he said. "Garnell told me he was real shocked to see the ball coming." Apparently,

the two principals hadn't even decided on the play.

Burns admitted that as the ball was in the air, "I was saying to myself, 'Please catch this ball because Coach Beamer is going to have my head if you don't.'" If Wilds hadn't caught the ball, Burns said, "I was going to keep on running into the end zone then right on home."

But Wilds did catch the ball on a 33-yard catch-and-run that was the most successful Hokie trick play that was never called.

Scam artists are everywhere — and they love trick plays. An e-mail encourages you to send money to some foreign country to get rich. That guy at your front door offers to resurface your driveway at a ridiculously low price. A TV ad promises a pill to help you lose weight without diet or exercise.

You've been around; you check things out before deciding. The same approach is necessary with spiritual matters, too, because false religions and bogus Christian denominations abound. The key is what any group does with Jesus. Is he the son of God, the ruler of the universe, and the only way to salvation? If not, then what the group espouses is something other than the true Word of God.

The good news about Jesus does indeed sound too good to be true. But the only catch is that there is no catch.

No trick -- just the truth.

That's why you recruit good players; sometimes they can overcome coaching.

-- Frank Beamer on the trick play that wasn't called

God's promises through Jesus sound too good to
be true, but the only catch is that there is no catch.

DAY 14

FOOD FOR THOUGHT

Read Genesis 9:1-7.

"Everything that lives and moves will be food for you. Just as I gave you the green plants, I now give you everything" (v. 3).

Dave Kadela once had to follow a very strict diet: Eat whatever he could get his hands on whenever he could.

Kadela was a mighty big man by the time he completed his football eligibility at Tech in 2000, standing 6-foot-6 and weighing 295 pounds. He played some as a freshman in 1997 and then started 34 straight games for the Hokies at right tackle. He was first-team All-Big East as a senior. "Dave is such a hard worker," praised offensive line coach Bryan Stinespring prior to the 2000 season. "He's always doing something to get better."

Once upon a time, that hard work and "doing something" to get better included eating. Actually, it went beyond eating. "I lived by the rule: Force feed when possible," Kadela said. That was after he came out of high school and was, to put it kindly, skinny. He was already 6'6" but he weighed only 210 pounds. He worked out at a hometown gym in high school and wound up lifting with the women. "The women there were as strong as I was," Kadela said.

Kedala drew little interest from colleges looking for football players and decided to spend a year at Fork Union Military Academy. There, an unorthodox diet of countless peanut butter and honey sandwiches and some serious weightlifting upped his

weight to 250 pounds and drew interest from the Hokies.

Strength and conditioning coach Mike Gentry took Kadela on as a project. His instructions included three orders of business: 1) eat; 2) eat again; 3) eat some more. Kadela "ate a ton of fast food, just sandwiches around the house. Whatever I could get my hands on, just eat all the time. I just inhaled food."

And ate his way into an all-conference career.

Belly up to the buffet, boys and girls, for barbecue, sirloin steak, grilled chicken, and fried catfish with hush puppies and cheese grits. Rachael Ray's a household name; hamburger joints, pizza parlors, and taco stands lurk on every corner; and we have a TV channel devoted exclusively to food. We love our chow.

Food is one of God's really good ideas, but consider the complex divine plan that begins with a seed and ends with French fries. The creator of all life devised a system in which living things are sustained and nourished physically through the sacrifice of other living things in a way similar to what Christ underwent to save us spiritually. Whether it's fast food or home-cooked, everything we eat is a gift from God secured through a divine plan in which some plants and animals have given up their lives.

Pausing to give thanks before we dive in seems the least we can do.

I cut down to six meals a day.

-- Charles Barkley on losing weight

**God created a system that nourishes us
through the sacrifice of other living things;
that's worth a thank-you.**

GREAT EXPECTATIONS

Read John 1:43-51.

*"'Nazareth! Can anything good come from there?'
Nathanael asked" (v. 46).*

The Hokie softball team had rather modest expectations for an exhibition game: Have a little fun and maybe last the full seven innings before getting beat. Instead, they pulled off one of the most incredible feats in the history of amateur softball.

On March 26, 2008, the Virginia Tech team was the sacrificial lamb *du jour* for the U.S. national softball team, which was in the midst of a pre-Olympic exhibition tour. After all, this was a team that had won 185 straight pre-Olympic exhibition games and had outscored its opponents 174-3 so far that year. The U.S. Olympic softball team had never in history lost to a true college team.

Before their game, the Hokies watched the U.S. team crush De-Paul 23-0 in five innings. The Hokies expected little better; perhaps they should have. They didn't just play the U.S. team close; they beat them 1-0, the first time the U.S. team had been shut out in any game since 2005. But there's more. Tech's All-American senior Angela Tincher didn't just shut out the U.S. team; she no-hit them. And the Hokies beat Jennie Finch, probably the most famous softball player in the country.

When Hokie shortstop Jess Hodge caught a pop up for the final out, Tincher's reaction was pretty much like everyone else's. "Did that just happen?" she thought in total shock. When Tech catcher

Kelsey Hoffman popped a double off Finch in the second inning, she paused in shock at the plate. "I was like, 'Oh, I just got a hit off Jennie Finch. I guess I should run now.'" Pinch runner Anna Zitt moved to third on an illegal pitch and then scored on a bloop single by outfielder Caroline Stolle.

The 2008 national player of the year and certainly the greatest player in Tech softball history, Tincher had tried out for that same Olympic team in 2007 and hadn't made the roster. Big mistake.

The blind date your friend promised would look like Brad Pitt or Jennifer Aniston but resembled Cousin Itt. Your vacation that went downhill after the lost luggage. Often your expectations are raised only to be dashed. Sometimes it's best not to get your hopes up; then at least you have the possibility of being surprised.

Worst of all, perhaps, is when you realize that you are the one not meeting others' expectations. The fact is, though, that you aren't here to live up to what others think of you. Jesus didn't; in part, that's why they killed him. But he did meet God's expectations for his life, which was all that really mattered.

Because God's kingdom is so great, God does have great expectations for any who would enter, and you should not take them lightly. What the world expects from you is of no importance; what God expects from you is paramount.

Getting to play them was a great experience. And to win? Ridiculous.
-- Angela Tincher on the win over the U.S. team

You have little if anything to gain
from meeting the world's expectations of you; you
have all of eternity to gain from meeting God's.

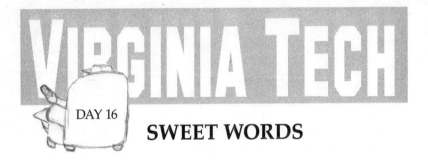

SWEET WORDS

Read John 8:1-11.

"'Then neither do I condemn you,' Jesus declared. 'Go now and leave your life of sin'" (v. 11).

Tech's head football coach was yet to have a winning season, but school officials nevertheless affirmed what he was doing by giving him an eight-year extension on his contract.

Frank Moseley arrived in Blacksburg in 1951 to turn around a football program that had won one game over the last three seasons. (See Devotion No. 90.) He won his first game, 18-12 over Marshall, but then the Hokies fell back into their losing ways, dropping seven straight on the way to a 2-8 season.

In 1952, though, Tech went 5-6, the most wins since 1942. Athletic officials were so excited and so sure about the direction of the program that before the 1953 season, they gave Moseley a new eight-year contract as coach and athletic director.

Not everyone was so sure after the 1953 season, however. The Hokies were 5-4 with only VMI left. Expecting an easy win and the first winning season since 1942, two of the leaders of the Virginia Tech Student Aid Foundation invited Owen Cheatham, the president of Georgia Pacific, to the game in hopes of impressing him into making a sizable contribution. They also bragged about the progress the program was making under Moseley

But their strategy backfired when VMI thoroughly whipped Tech 28-13. Cheatham was furious, subsequently had a heated

argument with Moseley, and determined to have him fired. Only after further conversations with the boosters did the frustrated Cheatham change his mind and agree the program was headed in the right direction under Moseley.

The administration's affirmation of Moseley with that new contract proved to be justified when Tech went undefeated in 1954, finishing the year ranked No. 16. The Hokies were back.

You make a key decision. All excited, you tell your best friend or spouse and anxiously await for a reaction. "Boy, that was dumb" is the answer you get. A friend's life spirals out of control into disaster. Alcohol, affairs, drugs, unemployment. Do you pretend you don't know that messed-up person?

Everybody needs affirmation in some degree. Even head football coaches. That is, we all occasionally need someone to say something positive about us, that we are worth something, and that God loves us.

The follower of Jesus does what our Lord did when he encountered someone whose life was a shambles. Rather than seeing what they were, he saw what they could become. Life is hard; it breaks us all to some degree. To be like Jesus, we see past the problems of the broken and the hurting and envision their potential, understanding that not condemning is not condoning.

You can motivate players better with kind words than you can with a whip.
-- Legendary college football coach Bud Wilkinson

**The greatest way to affirm lost persons
is to lead them to Christ.**

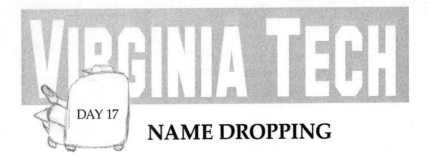
DAY 17

NAME DROPPING

Read Exodus 3:13-20.

"God said to Moses, 'I AM WHO I AM. This is what you are to say to the Israelites: 'I AM has sent me to you'" (v. 14).

Victor Lome Harris, Jr. has one of the great nicknames for a football player, one so identified with him that not even his family has ever called him by his Christian name. His nickname, did not, however, as might be expected, come about because of his superb play on the gridiron.

Harris finished his career at Tech in 2008 as one of the school's most versatile athletes ever. His senior season, for instance, he lined up at two different cornerback positions and at free safety. He also returned punts and kickoffs. Completing the trifecta, he rushed the ball a few times and nabbed several passes as a receiver. Harris "does everything for them," said Boston College had coach Jeff Jagodzinski.

As a junior in 2007, Harris was first-team All-ACC. He had five career touchdowns with Tech including a 72-yard interception return against Cincinnati in 2006 and a school-record 100-yard kickoff return against Clemson in 2007. He had fifteen career interceptions at Blacksburg and tied the ACC record by returning four interceptions for touchdowns.

And that nickname that is so appropriate for a tough football player? Macho. He is known as Macho Harris. Even the Virginia

Tech press releases referred to him as "Macho."

The nickname wasn't late in showing up; Harris has worn it virtually all his life. "I got it from my dad," Harris said about his moniker. "He came up with Macho and it [has] stuck with me ever since. I don't ever remember, not one time, somebody calling me Victor. Not my Mom or my family. Nobody called me that."

As in Macho Harris' case, nicknames are not slapped haphazardly upon individuals but often reflect widely held perceptions about the person named. Proper names do that also.

Nowhere throughout history has this concept been more prevalent than in the Bible, where a name is not a mere label but is an expression of the essential nature of the named one. That is, a person's name reveals his or her character. Even God shares this concept; to know the name of God is to know God as he has chosen to reveal himself to us.

What does your name say about you? Honest, trustworthy, a seeker of the truth and a person of God? Or does the mention of your name cause your coworkers to whisper snide remarks, your neighbors to roll their eyes, or your friends to start making allowances for you?

Most importantly, what does your name say about you to God? He, too, knows you by name.

He wanted to name me a masculine name.
      -- Macho Harris on his dad's choice of a nickname for him

**Live so that your name evokes
positive associations by people you know,
by the public, and by God.**

THE GOOD OLD DAYS

Read Psalm 102.

*"My days vanish like smoke; . . . but you remain the same,
and your years will never end" (vv. 3, 27).*

Once upon a time in a simpler day and age, in a time many may well regard as the "good old days" of Virginia Tech football, the Hokies and their fans enjoyed an annual football-related celebration and tradition that have not been equalled since.

Tech and VMI first played each other in 1894. Beginning in 1896 and continuing through 1969 with only a few exceptions, the two schools played each other on Thanksgiving Day in Roanoke in what became known as the "Military Classic of the South."

As one writer put it, the "Hokies always felt a comradeship with VMI, located only about 60 miles away in Lexington, because Tech originally required all students to join the Corps of Cadets." Over the years, though, the Military Classic "grew into more than a game; it became an event, the centerpiece of a holiday celebration, the city's official start to the Christmas shopping season."

The series hit the big time when it moved to brand new Victory Stadium in 1942. It was now "the biggest football game played in the state of Virginia," recalled former VMI coach John McKenna. Thousands of fans poured into Roanoke with full orchestras serenading them in downtown hotel lobbies and stores selling fur coats to women just for the game. Wrote *The Roanoke Times*, "It was a curious but successful mixture of old home week, Mardi

Gras and Christmas five weeks early." The *Times* sent out society writers to describe what the women in the stands wore. On game day, the Corps of Cadets from each school marched impressively through downtown Roanoke to the stadium.

Gradually, though, the rivalry faded as VMI remained a small military school and Tech burgeoned into a state university. The 1970 game was played on Saturday and marked the last game at Victory Stadium. The series was discontinued after the 1984 season. With it went a beautiful part of the "good old days."

It's a brutal truth that time just never stands still. The current of your life sweeps you along until you realize one day you've lived long enough to have a past. Part of it you cling to fondly. Your first apartment. That dance with your first love. That special vacation. The good times with your buddies. Those "good old days."

You hold on relentlessly to the memory of those old, familiar ways because of the stability they provide in our uncertain world. They will always be there even as times change and you age.

Another constant exists in your life too. God has been a part of every event in your life that created a memory because he was there. He's always there with you; the question is whether you ignore him or make him a part of your day.

A "good old day" is any day shared with God.

I'll always remember the VMI-VPI games. That was about as big as it got for a kid from Hillsville, Virginia.

--Frank Beamer

Today is one of the "good old days"
if you share it with God.

HANGING IN THERE

Read Mark 14:32-42.

"'Father,' he said, 'everything is possible for you. Take this cup from me. Yet not what I will, but what you will'" (v. 36).

We have a stick-to-itiveness." So did Tech men's basketball head coach Seth Greenberg succinctly sum up what lay behind a remarkable and downright stunning comeback.

On Jan. 28, 2010, the Hokies were on the road against archival Virginia, and -- to put it mildly -- things weren't looking any too good. "Not many people are winning on the road in the ACC," pointed out All-ACC guard Malcolm Delaney. That was a problem right there. Another serious problem developed with 13:41 to go when junior forward Jeff Allen was ejected on a questionable flagrant foul call. Virginia promptly ripped off ten straight points. Extremely problematic for Hokie fans was that as the clock inevitably ticked on, the Cavaliers held tightly onto that ten-point lead.

Still, the Hokies never gave up. "Everytime we huddled up, somebody said, 'We're still in it,'" said junior J.T. Thompson, Allen's backup, who exploded for 17 points. That persistence, though, appeared to accomplish only keeping UVa from pulling away. With 3:44 to go, Virginia led 62-52. At that point, Greenberg ordered a full-court press, and the Hokies took over. Delaney scored four points; Thompson added a bucket, and junior guard

Dorenzo Hudson buried a 3-pointer. When Thompson drove to the basket with 39 seconds left, Tech suddenly led 63-62.

The lead went to 65-62, and Tech appeared to have the win, but UVa nailed a trey with only 1:3 seconds left to send the game into overtime. The Hokies could have been disheartened, but instead they remained persistent, scoring the first five points in OT and never trailing again. They stuck to it and claimed an unlikely 76-71 win on their way to a 25-9 season and the NIT quarterfinals.

Life is tough; it inevitably beats us up and kicks us around some. But life has four quarters, and so here we are, still standing, still in the game. Like the Hokies against Virginia, we know that we can never win if we don't finish. We emerge as winners and champions only if we never give up, if we just see it through.

Interestingly, Jesus has been in the same situation. On that awful night in the garden, Jesus understood the nature of the suffering he was about to undergo, and he begged God to take it from him. In the end, though, he yielded to God's will and surrendered his own.

Even in the matter of persistence, Jesus is our example. As he did, we push doggedly and determinedly ahead – following God's will for our lives -- no matter how hard it gets. And we can do it because God is with us.

Never give up and sit down and grieve. Find another way.
– Satchel Paige

It's tough to keep going no matter what,
but you have the power of almighty God
to pull you through.

THE REWARD

Read 1 Corinthians 3:10-17.

"If what he has built survives, he will receive his reward" (v. 14).

When Tech beat Virginia 20-17 in the finale of the 1993 season with both teams heading for a bowl game, the logical conclusion to draw would be that the Hokies would be rewarded with a "bigger" bowl than the Cavs. Didn't happen.

As history unwound itself, the 1993 season may well have been the most important in the history of Tech football. Frank Beamer was in trouble; his six-year record as head coach in Blacksburg was 24-40-2, and the 1992 team had been a dismal 2-8-1. Wholesale changes in the Tech coaching staff were made. The result was an 8-3 regular season that served as the springboard to the national prominence that Tech has enjoyed under Beamer ever since.

The Hokies carried a 7-3 record into the Virginia game. Junior quarterback Maurice DeShazo, who Beamer called "the best option quarterback in the country," was the team's offensive leader. In addition to running the option, he set a school record with 22 touchdown passes.

The UVa game was an instant classic. Tech took a 17-3 lead behind the play of the defense. Freshman defensive end Cornell Brown sacked the Cav quarterback and caused a fumble, which tackle Jeff Holland scooped up and returned eight yards for a touchdown. In the third quarter, Virginia trailed only 17-10 and

faced fourth and one at the Hokie three. Virginia went for it, and freshman rover Torrian Gray stopped the play for no gain.

Tech finished 8-3 while Virginia was 7-4. Tech's reward for the win, though, was not what everyone expected. The Hokies wound up in the Independence Bowl with its $700,000 payoff, while UVa played in the Carquest Bowl with a $1 million payday. Irritation at the bowl situation was soothed somewhat when Tech blasted Indiana 45-20 and Boston College buried Virginia 31-13.

We want our rewards now. Hire a new football coach; he better win right away. You want to keep me happy? Then let's see a raise and a promotion immediately or I'm looking for another job. Want that new car or big house you can't afford? Hey that's what they make credit for, so I can live the good life today without having to pay for it now.

Jesus spoke often about rewards, but always in terms of eternal salvation and service to others rather than instant gratification or self-aggrandizement. The reward Jesus has in mind for us is the inevitable result of the way of life Jesus taught. To live with faith in God and in service to others is to move surely – if not swiftly – toward the eternal rewards included in our salvation.

The world's ephemeral material rewards may pass us by if we don't grab them right now. God's eternal spiritual rewards, however, will absolutely be ours.

The price of victory is high but so are the rewards.

-- *Bear Bryant*

God rewards our faith, patience, and service by fulfilling the promises he has made to us.

DAY 21

ANIMAL MAGNETISM

Read Psalm 139:1-18.

"For you created my inmost being; you knit me together in my mother's womb. I praise you because I am fearfully and wonderfully made" (vv. 13-14).

Virginia Tech's early mascots had rather lousy rewards for a season of service to the football team: They were eaten for dinner.

A youth named Floyd Meade was responsible for the first mascot for what was popularly known from 1896 on as Virginia Polytechnic Institute or VPI. Meade lived with the family of cadet N. W. Thomas and became a favorite in the barracks. Cadets nicknamed him "Hard Times."

As a teenager, Meade dressed up as a clown and performed at football games in the manner of a one-man band. Tiring of that, he began to feed and train a turkey to gobble on command. He billed his bird as "the largest in Montgomery County."

Tech's original mascot introduced his new mascot at the first football game of the 1912 season. Meade dressed in a three-piece suit, hitched his big turkey to a small, two-wheeled cart, rode around in the cart pulled by the turkey. With one quite bizarre performance, Meade reinforced the school's two nicknames: the Hokies from an 1896 cheer, and Gobblers, which had become a popular reference to the school's athletic teams around 1908.

The school president declared pulling the cart to be cruelty to animals, so Meade ditched it after one game. He continued, how-

ever, to bring live turkeys to games with each mascot winding up as the main course for dinner at season's end. He eventually passed the tradition on to Joe "Chesty" Price, who raised the birds and showcased them on the sideline until he retired in 1953.

The first permanent costumed Gobbler showed up in 1962, but the nickname was not destined to last after a head football coach in the late 1970s preferred the "Hokie" image. The costume was changed in 1982 to resemble a maroon cardinal rather than a turkey. Today's HokieBird costume first appeared in 1987.

Nothing enlivens a trip more than glimpsing turkeys, bears, or deer in the wild. Admit it: You go along with the kids' trip to the zoo because you think it's a cool place too. All that variety of life is mind-boggling. Who could conceive of a turkey, a moose, or a prairie dog? Who could possibly have that rich an imagination?

But the next time you're in a crowd, look around at the parade of faces. Who could come up with the idea for all those different people? For that matter, who could conceive of you? You are unique, a masterpiece who will never be duplicated.

The master creator, God Almighty, is behind it all. He thought of you and brought you into being. If you had a manufacturer's label, it might say, "Lovingly, fearfully, and wonderfully handmade in Heaven by #1 -- God."

One story claimed the term "Gobbler" was coined in the early 1900s as a description of how student athletes "gobbled" up their food servings.
-- "From Gobbler to Hokiebird"

**You may consider a painting or a beautiful animal
a work of art, but the real masterpiece is you.**

THE PANIC BUTTON

Read Mark 4:35-41.

"He said to his disciples, 'Why are you so afraid? Do you still have no faith?'" (v. 40).

For Virginia Tech fans, the time had come to panic.

On Nov. 6, 1999, the undefeated Hokies took on 3-5 West Virginia with a chance at the national championship on the line, especially when No. 2 Penn State was upset prior to kickoff. A spot in the title game was there for the Hokies to take.

Michael Vick's 51-yard pass to Andre Davis set up a six-yard TD run by Shyrone Stith to give Tech a 19-7 lead with only 4:59 to play. But after a good kickoff return, West Virginia used only four plays to score. With 3:15 on the clock, Tech led only 19-14.

No reason to panic yet, though, as the Hokies set about the business of running the clock out -- until they fumbled. Once again, the Mountaineers took only four plays to score. With only 1:15 on the clock, West Virginia suddenly led 20-19.

Now was quite certainly a perfect time to panic.

The fans may have become frenzied, but the Hokie players didn't panic. While West Virginia was going in for the score, offensive coordinator Rickey Bustle was having a serious conversation with Vick aimed at keeping his quarterback calm. They reviewed the team's two-minute drill and which plays would work best. One of the last things Bustle told Vick was, "Don't forget; you can always pull it down and run."

With time running out, Vick did just that, rolling to his right and scrambling for 26 yards to the West Virginia 36. He then hit Ricky Hall for nine more yards and spiked the ball with five seconds left. As calm as his offense had been, Shayne Graham kicked the field goal for the 22-20 win.

Have you ever experienced that suffocating sensation of fear escalating into full-blown panic? Maybe the time when you couldn't find your child at the mall or at the beach? Or the heart-stopping moment when you looked out and saw that tornado headed your way?

As the disciples illustrate, the problem with panic is that it debilitates us. Here they were, professional fishermen in the bunch, and they let a bad storm panic them into helplessness. All they could do was wake up an exhausted Jesus.

We shouldn't be too hard on them, though, because we often make the same mistake they did when we encounter a situation fraught with danger and fear. That is, we underestimate both Jesus' power and his ability to handle our crises.

We have a choice when fear clutches us: We can assume Jesus no longer cares for us, surrender to it, and descend into panic, or we can remember how much Jesus loves us and resist fear and panic by trusting in him.

I'll tell you what I said. I said a prayer.
-- Frank Beamer on what he said to Shayne Graham before his field goal

To plunge into panic is to believe
– quite wrongly -- that Jesus is incapable
of handling the crises in our lives.

LIMITED-TIME OFFER

Read Psalm 103.

"As for man, his days are like grass, he flourishes like a flower of the field; the wind blows over it and it is gone. . . . But from everlasting to everlasting the Lord's love is with those who fear him" (vv. 15-17).

His has been called "the greatest and saddest of Tech football stories." He was safety Frank Loria, Virginia Tech's first consensus All-America, which was the "greatest" part; his untimely death at a young age in a plane crash was the "saddest" part.

According to the experts, Loria was too small and too slow for major college football. But what Loria didn't have physically he more than made up for with "the instincts, the fearlessness, and, above all, . . . a nearly insatiable need to put the big chill on a ball carrier," traits that are absolutely necessary for a great defensive back. He stood only 5-foot-9 and weighed only 179 pounds, but Tech legend Mac McEver, who helped with the defensive backs at the time, said Loria was so good he should have gotten two letters: one for linebacker and one for safety.

Loria was the star of the great 1966 defense, "That defense hurt people," said Tech offensive end Ken Barefoot. "We used to hate to scrimmage against them in practice." Head coach Jerry Claiborne's practices were physical with the coaches constantly in the players' faces. But, recalled Barefoot, they "left Loria alone because he always knew what he was doing."

He was Tech's first consensus All-America in 1966, the season of the Hokies' first of two trips to the Liberty Bowl. As a senior in 1967, Loria was named to the top seven All-America first teams. He was also a two-time Academic All-America.

The pros ignored him in the 1968 draft, and Loria eventually joined the coaching staff at Marshall. He was aboard the DC-9 that crashed after a game on Nov. 14, 1970, killing everyone aboard.

A plane crash, car wreck, or some other kind of accident or an illness or disease such as a heart attack, or cancer will probably take -- or has already taken -- someone you know or love who is "too young to die" such as Frank Loria. The death of a young person never seems to make sense because such a death belies the common view of death as the natural end of a life lived well and lived long. Moreover, you can't see the whole picture as God does, so you can't know how the death furthers God's kingdom.

At such a time, you can seize the comforting truth that God is in control and therefore everything will be all right one day. You can also gain a sense of urgency in your own life by appreciating that God's offer of life through Jesus Christ is a limited-time offer that expires at your death – and there's no guarantee about when that will be.

No one knows when he is going to die, so if we're going to accept Christ, we'd better not wait because death might come in the blink of an eye.
-- Bobby Bowden

God offers you life through Jesus Christ,
but you must accept the offer before your death,
which is when it expires.

IMPORTANT STUFF

Read Matthew 6:25-34.

"Seek first his kingdom and his righteousness, and all these things will be given to you as well" (v. 33).

Spyridon Jullien had to get his priorities in line: the violin or his sport. Fortunately for Virginia Tech, the violin lost out.

Simply put, Jullien is the most successful and most decorated athlete in Tech history though many fans may never have heard of him. In 2005 and 2006, Jullien brought to Virginia Tech what at the time no other Hokie had before: a national championship. And he brought four of them. Jullien won the national title both years in the NCAA Indoor and Outdoor Track and Field Championships -- in the hammer throw. Among Jullien's countless awards, he is the only athlete in Tech history to twice be named the Male Athlete of the Year.

Jullien grew up in Greece wrestling, fencing, and throwing for a sports club as a teenager. He focused on the discus, shot put, and javelin until he saw someone practicing the hammer throw. "I said, 'That's it,'" he recalled. "It was beautiful. I was charmed."

Jullien became so proficient at it that he drew the attention of Tech throws coach Greg Jack. The coach sent the young Greek an e-mail asking him if he'd like to join the Hokies. "I had no idea Virginia Tech existed before being contacted" by Jack, Jullien said. But he figured he would give it a try since he wasn't particularly happy at the time as a freshman at a college in northern Greece.

The rest is Virginia Tech sports history.

About that violin. Jullien started playing when he was 9 years old, but his dedication to the hammer throw forced him to make a choice. "My arms became too stiff and my hands really full of calluses," he said. So he decided what his priority was: "I stopped the violin because of the hammer."

Playing the violin or throwing around an extremely awkward track and field utensil may not be the most important thing in your life, but you do have priorities. What is it that you would surrender only with your dying breath? Your family? Every dime you have? Your Hokie season tickets?

What about God? Would you denounce your faith in Jesus Christ rather than lose your children? Or everything you own?

God doesn't force us to make such unspeakable choices; nevertheless, followers of Jesus Christ often become confused about their priorities because so much in our lives clamors for attention and time. It all seems so worthwhile.

But Jesus' instructions are unequivocal: Seek God first. Turn to him first for help, fill your thoughts with what he wants for you and your life, use God's character as revealed in Jesus as the pattern for everything you do, and serve and obey him in all matters, at all moments.

God – and God alone – is No. 1.

If you've ever heard me at a press conference, the first thing I do is give honor to God because he's first in my life.
-- College basketball coach Gary Waters

God should always be number one in our lives.

DAY 25

THE LEADER

Read Matthew 16:18-23.

"You are Peter, and on this rock I will build my church, and the gates of Hades will not overcome it" (v. 18).

The Hokies were young and discouraged and on the verge of having their season collapse. And then their leader stepped up.

In its first season in the ACC, the 2004 Tech football team was 5-2 and on a three-game win streak when it traveled to Atlanta for an Oct. 28 game against Georgia Tech. The Jackets promptly jumped out to a 14-0 lead in the first quarter and spent the rest of the half pretty much pounding the Hokies.

The mood in the locker room at halftime was somewhat less than upbeat. "I remember going into the locker room, everybody was down, thinking the season was going downhill," recalled freshman receiver Eddie Royal. But Va. Tech had on its team a senior quarterback named Bryan Randall. He set a school record with 38 straight starts at quarterback, and that 2004 season, he was the ACC Player of the Year. Randall also had invaluable attributes beyond his abundant physical skills: He was a born leader.

Randall used those leadership skills in that morose halftime locker room to encourage the young players and keep them in the game. "I didn't actually give a talk," Randall said. "I was walking around the locker room, telling everybody to keep their heads up. I was just telling people, 'We're going to get it done.'"

It worked. The Hokies hung around, trailing 20-12 in the fourth

quarter. Then Randall hit Royal with an 80-yard touchdown pass and Josh Morgan for a 51-yard score in only 1:16. A Roland Minor interception made the final score 34-20. The Hokies went on to win the rest of their regular-season games and the ACC title -- thanks in large part to their leader on and off the field.

Every aspect of life that involves people – every organization, every group, every project, every team -- must have a leader. If goals are to be reached, somebody must take charge.

Even the early Christian church was no different. Jesus knew this, so he designated the leader in Simon Peter, who was such an unlikely choice to assume such an awesome, world-changing responsibility that Jesus soon after rebuked him as "Satan."

In his *Twelve Ordinary Men*, John MacArthur described Simon as "ambivalent, vacillating, impulsive, unsubmissive." Hardly a man to inspire confidence in his leadership skills. Yet, Peter became, according to MacArthur, "the greatest preacher among the apostles" and the "dominant figure" in the birth of the church.

The implication for your own life is both obvious and unsettling. You may think you lack the attributes necessary to make a good leader for Christ. But consider Simon Peter, an ordinary man who allowed Christ to rule his life and became the foundation upon which the Christian church was built.

A lot of people think a good player is going to be a good leader, which is not true.

-- Bryan Randall

God's leaders are men and women
who allow Jesus to lead them.

DANCING MACHINE

Read 2 Samuel 6:12-22.

"David danced before the Lord with all his might, while he and the entire house of Israel brought up the ark of the Lord with shouts and the sound of trumpets" (vv. 14-15).

The rally was so sudden and so surprising that it turned head coach Frank Beamer into a dancing machine in the locker room after the game.

On Sept. 20, 2008, North Carolina led the Hokies 17-3 midway through the third quarter. The Tech offense was doing little; the defense had just been gashed for a 50-yard touchdown run. The Hokies "were cooked. They were done." "It didn't look too good for us, that's for certain," said tailback Darren Evans. Then in 5:27, the Hokies turned it all around, putting up 17 points and snatching a 20-17 win away from certain defeat.

It all started with a big third-down play. Tech faced third and 7 at its own 17, not exactly a promising scenario since the Hokies were 1-for-10 on third-down chances in the game. But quarterback Tyrod Taylor scrambled and hit freshman wideout Dyrell Roberts for a 15-yard completion. That seemed to fire up the dormant offense, which proceeded to march downfield and score on Evans' 10-yard run up the middle.

On the second play after the kickoff, defensive end Orion Martin forced a fumble that Davon Morgan recovered at the Heel 30. Five plays later, Kenny Lewis scored from the 11. With 13:46 to

play, the game was tied at 17. With 10:42 left, Dustin Keys booted a 45-yard field goal that was the difference.

Interceptions from Macho Harris and Stephan Virgil sealed the second biggest comeback in Beamer's tenure and set him to celebrating with his "Fancy Gap Frank" jig. "The boys like my dancing," Beamer said with a grin in the boisterous locker room.

One of the more enduring stereotypes of the Christian is of a dour, sour-faced person always on the prowl to sniff out fun and frivolity and shut it down. "Somewhere, sometime, somebody's having fun – and it's got to stop!" Many understand this to be the mandate that governs the Christian life.

But nothing could be further from reality. Ages ago King David, he who would eventually number Jesus Christ among his house and lineage, set the standard for those who love and worship the Lord when he danced in the presence of God with unrestrained joy. Many centuries and one savior later, David's example today reminds us that a life spent in an awareness of God's presence is all about celebrating, rejoicing, and enjoying God's countless gifts, including salvation in Jesus Christ.

Yes, dancing can be vulgar and coarse, but as with David, God looks into our hearts to see what is there. Our very life should be one long song and dance for Jesus.

Oh, my gosh, I've never seen Coach Beamer like that before.
-- Senior kicker Dustin Keys on his dancing head coach

While dancing and music can be vulgar
and obscene, they can also be inspiring
expressions of abiding love for God.

A CASE OF THE NERVES

Read Mark 5-1-20.

""What do you want with me, Jesus, Son of the Most High God? Swear to God that you won't torture me!" (v. 7)

The kicker whose last-second field goal propelled the Hokies to their first-ever bowl win admitted that he got nervous about his pressure-packed kicks only days later when he watched the game tapes.

As the Hokie place kicker from 1985-88, Chris Kinzer fulfilled his lifelong dream of playing football for Virginia Tech. He set school records in 1986 by making seventeen field goals in a row and 22 for the season. The Associated Press named him second-team All-America that year.

While Kinzer is most remembered for his kick in the 1986 Peach Bowl, he also delivered against Kentucky during the season. With the Hokies trailing 15-14 and running out of time, quarterback Eric Chapman moved the team downfield. As the clock wound down, Kinzer boomed a 50-yard field goal for the 17-15 win.

Equally dramatic was his kick in the Peach Bowl after the 8-2-1 Hokie regular season. N.C. State led 24-22 with the clock racing toward zero when Kinzer did it again, this time from 40 yards out. The 25-24 win was Tech's first-ever in a bowl game.

As his game-winning kicks demonstrate, being nervous was not a problem for Kinzer. At least not while the game was on

the line and tens of thousands of people were screaming at him and praying he would fail. Strangely enough, Kinzer collapsed into a nervous wreck only when he got back home in Virginia and watched the game tapes "even though I already knew the outcome." "I couldn't believe how nervous I was," he said.

Like Chris Kinzer and his case of the nerves long after the pressurized moment had passed, we often can't really explain why some situations make us nervous. Making a speech, for instance. Or being in the presence of a person we'd like to ask out.

We probably rarely if ever consider the possibility that we make other people nervous. Who in the world could be intimidated by us? Try this on for starters: Satan himself. Yep, that very demon of darkness that Hollywood repeatedly portrays as so powerful that goodness is helpless before him. That's the one.

But we can make Satan nervous only if we stand before him with the power of Jesus Christ at our disposal. As Christians, we seem to understand that our basic mission is to further Jesus' kingdom and change the world through emulating him in the way we live and love others. But do we appreciate that in truly living for Jesus, we are daily tormenting the very devil himself?

Satan and his lackeys quake helplessly in fear and nervousness before the power of almighty God that is in us through Jesus.

When you're out there on the field, playing, you're really not nervous because you're so focused on what you're doing.
-- Chris Kinzer

**Nervous and apprehensive -- so stands Satan
himself in the presence of a follower of Jesus.**

BE PREPARED

Read Matthew 10:5-23.

*"I am sending you out like sheep among wolves. Therefore
be as shrewd as snakes and as innocent as doves" (v. 16).*

Bobby Stevens prepared himself for basketball by using what
may well be the strangest practice technique ever. It paid off when
he hit what has been called "the most important buzzer-beater in
Virginia Tech history."

In 1973, Tech's squad finished 18-5 and received a surprise
invitation to the 16-team NIT. The Gobblers were viewed as inter-
lopers, "too small, too slow, and too Virginian" to win. But Tech
clipped favored New Mexico in the opener 65-63, edged Fairfield
(Conn.) 77-76 in the second round, and upset an athletic Alabama
team 74-73 in the semifinals. The surprising Hokies were in the
finals against Notre Dame.

The Irish led by one point with time running out. Stevens, a
5'-10" junior guard, missed a shot but ran down the loose ball only
to find himself covered by all 6'3" of Notre Dame's Willie Town-
send. He had no choice; he put the shot up. "I don't know how he
didn't block the shot," Stevens remembered. "He was all over me.
I couldn't see a thing."

But Stevens had prepared for just such a moment. Growing up,
he and a friend would turn out the gym lights and Stevens would
practice shooting in the dark. "I figured that someday I would
have to shoot over somebody so big that I wouldn't be able to see

the basket," he said, explaining his weird practice sessions.

That day had come. Without seeing the basket, he hit nothing but net as the buzzer sounded. Tech won 92-91; the Gobblers were the champions of the NIT because Bobby Stevens had prepared for just such a shot as the one against Notre Dame.

You know the importance of preparation in your own life. You went to the bank for a car loan, facts and figures in hand. That presentation you made at work was seamless because you practiced. The kids' school play suffered no meltdowns because they rehearsed. Knowing what you need to do and doing what you must to succeed isn't luck; it's preparation.

Jesus understood this, and he prepared his followers by lecturing them and by sending them on field trips. Two thousand years later, the life of faith requires similar training and study. You prepare so you'll be ready when that unsaved neighbor standing beside you at your backyard grill asks about Jesus. You prepare so you will know how God wants you to live. You prepare so you are certain in what you believe when the secular, godless world challenges it.

And one day you'll see God face to face. You certainly want to be prepared for that.

Spectacular achievements are always preceded by unspectacular preparation.

-- Roger Staubach

**Living in faith requires constant study
and training, preparation for the day
when you meet God face to face.**

CAN'T GO WRONG

Read Galatians 6:7-10.

"Let us not grow weary in doing what is right, for we will reap at harvest time, if we do not give up" (v. 9 NRSV).

Carroll Dale was successful because of the one simple but powerful approach he took to life, which included football: He always tried to do the right thing.

In 1959, Dale became Tech's first All-America football player. He was, quite simply, one of the greatest players in school history, a pass-catching end in a day before today's wide-open offenses. The *Saturday Evening Post* named him the top sophomore lineman in the country. As a junior in 1958, he was the Southern Conference Player of the Year, and *Look* magazine named him first-team All-America as a senior. He led the Hokies in receiving four straight seasons.

Dale originally committed to Tennessee in an age before the binding letter-of-intent existed. One visit to Blacksburg changed his mind, however. He was a small-town boy, and he liked the Tech setting. "Blacksburg was a much better fit for me," he said. "I would have much less temptation there, and be able to concentrate on the books. Not having a vehicle, I could get downtown easily or get to church."

That last remark reveals the secret to Dale's lifelong success. As he put it, growing up, he "was taken to church, not sent." He always has lived with a keen sense of a higher purpose in life. "I

really think the spiritual side of it kept me in line, trying to do the right thing," he once said.

John Moody (See Devotion No. 77.), Dale's partner at receiver and roommate, said his friend's outlook, based on a firm hold on his faith, was what gave him "an excellent work ethic" and made him "a great person, a great leader."

Carroll Dale's life is a testimony to doing the right thing.

Doing the right thing is easy when it's little stuff. Giving the quarter back when the cashier gives you too much change, helping a lost child at the mall, or putting a few bucks in the honor box at your favorite fishing hole.

But what about when it costs you? Every day you have multiple chances to do the right thing; in every instance, you have a choice: right or wrong. The factors that weigh into your decisions – including the personal cost to you – reveal much about your character.

Does your doing the right thing ever depend upon your calculation of the odds of getting caught? In the world's eyes, you can't go wrong doing wrong when you won't get caught. That passes for the world's slippery, situational ethics, but it doesn't pass muster with God.

In God's eyes, you can't go wrong doing right. Ever.

He was always going to class, always doing his homework, always had the Good Book with him.

-- John Moody on Carroll Dale

**As far as God is concerned,
you can never go wrong doing right.**

DAY 30

A SURE THING

Read Romans 8:28-30.

"We know that in all things God works for the good of those who love him, who have been called according to his purpose" (v. 28).

Once upon a time, relations between Virginia Tech and UVa were so strained by their football games that the Tech team left Blacksburg for the game not even sure it would be played.

From their first football meeting in 1895, the two schools regarded each other with mutual animosity. Their acrimony came to a head before the 1905 game over the eligibility of Tech's Hunter Carpenter, who was playing his seventh season in those days of loose rules. As the game neared, Virginia players began to grouse that Carpenter and others were actually professionals.

The week of the game, UVa's athletic managers announced they would not play the game unless Carpenter stood trial "before a jury of unprejudiced men." Tech head coach C.P. Miles scoffingly dismissed the whole notion. The Thursday before the game, the UVa officials notified Tech managers that the game was off and the guarantee of Tech's expense money was revoked.

Carpenter and the team turned to the student body and raised the traveling money. The squad then informed Virginia that they were coming to play the game anyway. "We left Blacksburg on Friday and went to Lynchburg by train," Miles recalled. "We took our meals in bags and ate in our [hotel] rooms so there would be

no trouble. But we still didn't know if the game would be played."
At the Hokies' team hotel, when a reporter asked Carpenter if the
game was on, he replied, "Certainly I expect to play."

But the game wasn't a sure thing even after the crowd packed
the field and the two teams showed up. They wrangled for a
while before Virginia relented and Carpenter led an 11-0 Tech
win, its first in the series. The relations between the two schools
had deteriorated so badly that they did not play again until 1923.

Football games aren't played on paper. That is, you attend a
Virginia Tech game expecting the Hokies to win, but you don't
know for sure. If you did, why bother to go? Any football game
worth watching carries with it an element of uncertainty.

Life doesn't get played on paper either, which means that
living, too, comes laden with uncertainty. You never know what's
going to happen tomorrow or even an hour from now. Oh, sure,
you think you know. For instance, right now you may be certain
that you'll be at work Monday morning or that you'll have a job
next month. Life's uncertainties, though, can intervene at any
time and disrupt your nice, pat expectations.

Ironically, while you can't know for sure about this afternoon,
you can know for certain about forever. Eternity is a sure thing because it's in God's hands. Your unwavering faith and God's sure
promises lock in a certain future for you.

There is nothing in life so uncertain as a sure thing.
-- NHL coach Scotty Bowman

**Life is unpredictable and tomorrow is uncertain;
eternity is a sure thing because God controls it.**

GOOD JOB

Read Matthew 25:14-30.

"His master replied, 'Well done, good and faithful servant!'" (v. 21)

Good job. What else is there to say about the day Brad Bauder had at the plate against Georgetown during the 2002 Hokie baseball season? Well, you could say you don't believe it, which would be a pretty reasonable statement.

Bauder was the starting center fielder for the Hokies on April 21 when they met Georgetown. He wasn't exactly on a hot streak, entering the game in a 10-for-54 slump (.185). He was only 2-for-9 in a doubleheader sweep of Georgetown on Saturday. Still, Bauder was encouraged. "I hit the ball hard" in both games, he said. "I knew things were going to start falling for me."

He had no idea.

What happened was one of the greatest days in NCAA baseball history. In a 35-4 embarrassment of Georgetown, Bauder went 8 -for-8, hit four home runs, and drove in 14 runs. In addition to his homers, he had two singles, a double, and a triple to complete the cycle. He set both Tech and Big East records for hits, RBIs, and total bases (23) in a game. In all three categories, he tied for the second-best output in college baseball history. He also scored seven runs to set a new Big East record and tie the school mark.

"Who can ever explain what happens to a guy like that?" Hokie head coach Chuck Hartman said after the game. "It's one of those

sports phenomena that I'm not sure you can explain." A college head coach since 1960, Hartman said he had never seen anyone go 8-for-8. "You think he'd pop one up or hit one in the ground or something like that."

But Brad Bauder never did. When he said he thought "things were going to fall for me" Sunday, he didn't think "they'd start falling over the fence." And everywhere else. But they did.

Good job. Well done. Way to go.

They are words that make us all swell up a little like a puffer fish and smile no matter how hard we try not to. We may deny it in an honest attempt to be at least reasonably humble, but we all cherish praise. We work hard and we may be well rewarded for it financially, but a cold, hard paycheck is not always enough. We like to be told we're doing something well; we desire to be appreciated.

Nowhere, however, is that affirmation more important than when it comes from God himself. We will all meet God one day, which is intimidating even to consider. How our soul will ring with unspeakable joy on that day of days if we hear God's thundering voice say to us, "Well done, good and faithful servant."

Could anything else really matter other than doing a good job for God?

Everyone keeps saying, 'How did you do it?' The only way I really did it was my team got 37 hits to get me up there eight times.
-- Brad Bauder on being asked how he got eight hits

If we don't do a good job for God in our lives,
all our work amounts to nothing.

DAY 32

FATHERS AND SONS

Read Luke 3:1-22.

"And a voice came from heaven: 'You are my Son, whom I love; with you I am well pleased'" (v. 22).

Rashad "Rock" Carmichael grew up in a big, extended family that included what he called "mostly ladies," but his father was always the one he turned to.

"My dad was everything to me," Carmichael once said. "He was my mentor, he was the one showed me the way. Man, I love him. He was the one who made me 'Rock.'" Quite literally. When the senior Carmichael heard all those ladies calling his oldest son "Ra Ra," he quickly put an end to that business, declaring the moniker to be too soft. His boy would be "Rock" from now on.

Carmichael was indeed solid as a rock for the Hokies. He was a starting cornerback in 2009 and 2010. He was named the ACC Defensive Back of the Week for his play in Tech's 49-27 defeat of East Carolina on Sept. 18, 2010. He had two interceptions in the game, returning one 68 yards for a touchdown. His success at Tech was right in keeping with the plan his father and he laid out. The only hitch was that Rock's dad wasn't around to see it.

In July 2008, 40-year-old Bernard Carmichael told his three boys that he didn't expect to live much longer because of high blood pressure. A few days later he called Rock at his apartment for a routine chat that ended with the dad's words, "I'll talk to you later." "I don't know why, but I just knew I wasn't going to talk to

him again," the son said.

He didn't. An hour later, his dad died from a heart attack. Rock refused to answer the phone when his mom called, forcing her to contact Jason Worilds, Carmichael's closest friend on the team. He delivered the awful news: Rock's father was gone.

Contemporary American society largely belittles and marginalizes fathers and their influence upon their sons. Men are perceived as necessary to effect pregnancy; after that, they can leave and everybody's better off.

But we need look in only two places to appreciate the enormity of that misconception: our jails – packed with males who lacked the influence of fathers in their lives as they grew up -- and the Bible. God – being God – could have chosen any relationship he desired between Jesus and himself, including society's approach of irrelevancy. Instead, the most important relationship in all of history was that of father-son.

God obviously believes a close, loving relationship between fathers and sons, such as that of Bernard and Rashad Carmichael, is crucial. For men and women to espouse otherwise or for men to walk blithely and carelessly out of their children's lives constitutes disobedience to the divine will.

Simply put, God loves fathers. After all, he is one.

I know my dad is happy. And one of these days down the road, we'll run into each other again.

— *Rashad 'Rock' Charmichael*

**Fatherhood is a tough job, but a model
for the father-child relationship is found in that
of Jesus the Son with God the Father.**

WORM DROWNING

Read Mark 1:16-20.

"'Come, follow me,' Jesus said, 'and I will make you fishers of men'" (v. 17).

Because Tommy Francisco's dad arranged for him to go fishing, Virginia Tech landed one of its greatest football players ever.

Francisco's six rushing touchdowns against VMI in 1966 broke a 44-year-old Tech single game record and still stands today. The senior tailback's school record of fourteen touchdowns that year lasted until Lee Suggs blew past it with 28 in 2000.

After a slow start, Coach Jerry Claiborne's '66 team ripped off six straight wins. Still, they entered the season-ending game against VMI with a chip on their collective shoulders. Despite their 7-1-1 record, the Hokies had thus far been shut out of the bowls. FSU, which Tech beat 23-21 had a bowl bid, but not the Hokies. VMI suffered their wrath on Nov. 24 in Roanoke in a 70-12 slaughter.

Francisco led the romp with his record-setting day. He scored on runs of 1, 26, 1, 3, 1, and 3 yards, finishing with 132 yards on 32 carries. (Tech subsequently received a bid to the Liberty Bowl.)

Francisco was a Hokie fan growing up, and to no one's surprise, he signed to play football for Tech. But Kentucky stayed after him, and when he made a visit to Lexington, he signed with the Wildcats. His parents were not one bit happy about that.

His dad solved the problem by lending his houseboat to the school. Some coaches showed up and took Tommy fishing. "We

just got out in the middle of the lake [and sat there]," he recalled. "I just loved to fish. I figured out later what was going on." Tommy's dad had no intentions of letting his son play football for anybody but Tech, so he had made sure his son was safely tucked away until it was time for him to head to Blacksburg.

The worst fishing trip you ever had may have included numbing cold, nary a nibble, a flat tire, or any combination of misadventures. You dragged in late, knowing full well you had to get up early next morning. Still, it was better than a good day at work, wasn't it?

What if somebody in authority looked you square in the eyes and told you, "Go Fish"? How quickly would you trip over anybody who got in your way? Well, Jesus did exactly that, commanding his followers to fish for people who are drowning and lost without him.

Jesus issued that command with the utmost seriousness. For the men of his time, fishing was neither for pleasure nor for sport. Rather, it was hard work, a demanding, hardscrabble way to support a family. Fishing for men and women for Jesus is likewise hard work, but it is such the essence of the Christian mission that a fish has become the symbol of the faith itself.

Some go to church and think about fishing; others go fishing and think about God.

-- *Fisherman Tony Blake*

**Jesus understood the passion people have
for fishing and commanded that it become
not just a hobby but a way of life.**

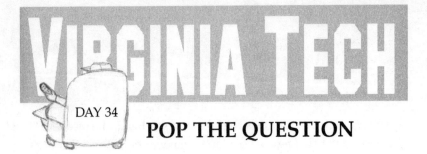

POP THE QUESTION

Read Matthew 16:13-17.

"'But what about you?' he asked. 'Who do you say I am?'" (v. 15)

Trailing by a bucket in the last half of a key conference game, the Hokies called time out. And that's when the question many in the home crowd sought an answer to changed from "Will Tech win?" to "Will she say 'yes'?"

Hokie fan Trace King decided to propose to his girlfriend of four years, Jennifer Trail, during the second time out of Virginia Tech's last home game before Valentine's Day 1997. A real problem lay in the Tech policy that forbade using scoreboards for marriage proposals. "We get many, many requests," explained Jack Williams, Tech's director of media relations. "We thought if we did one we'd have to do 30 a game."

But King's uncle, John Moody, an associate director of development in the athletic department, found some quite willing and quite excited accomplices in the Hokie cheerleaders. They put together a giant banner that read, "Jennifer, will you marry me? Love, Trace." The Hokie Bird was part of the plot, too, standing by with a sign that read "Yes" on one side and "No" on the other.

Everything was ready when Tech hosted George Washington on Feb. 5. The fateful moment came with 11:53 left to play: time out. There sat King, his parents, her parents, his aunts and uncles, and a cousin, and, of course, the clueless object of his affections.

The cheerleaders maneuvered into a pyramid and held up the sign. "Somebody's doing a marriage proposal," Jennifer thought. And then she saw King's name, "and my eyes got so big. I looked at him and he was teary-eyed and of course I got teary-eyed." In case she missed it, King was also down on one knee.

It was a good night all around. She said yes and Tech won.

Life is an ongoing search for answers, and thus whether our life is lived richly or is wasted is largely determined by both the quality and the quantity of the answers we find. Life is indeed one question after another. What's for dinner? Can we afford a new car? What kind of team will Tech have this season?

But we also continuously seek answers to questions at another, more crucial level. What will I do with my life? Why am I here? Why does God allow suffering and tragedy?

An aspect of wisdom is reconciling ourselves to and being comfortable with the fact that we will never know all the answers. Equally wise is the realization that the answers to life's more momentous questions lie within us, not beyond us.

One question overrides all others, the one Jesus asked Peter: "Who do you say I am?" Peter gave the one and only correct answer: "You are the Son of the Living God." How you answer that question is really the only one that matters, since it decides not just how you spend your life but how you spend eternity.

'Oh, my gosh, he's doing to do it.' 'Here?'
-- Two Tech students realizing Trace King was about to pop the question

Only one question in life determines
your eternal fate: Who do you say Jesus is?

DAY 35

PRECIOUS MEMORIES

Read 1 Thessalonians 3:6-13.

"Timothy . . . has brought good news about your faith and love. He has told us that you always have pleasant memories of us" (v. 6).

Outstanding Tech football player, the team's co-MVP, collegiate strength and conditioning coach, husband, and father -- Since he is or has been all of these things, Jimmy Whitten can't be certain how he will be remembered. He does know, though, how he does *not* want to be remembered: as the player who knocked out head coach Frank Beamer's tooth.

As a senior in 1990, Whitten, a defensive end, was named the team's co-MVP and the most valuable defensive lineman and received the Captain's Award. He had many great moments as a Tech player. His most infamous moment, however, occurred after the 1989 Virginia game when "within moments of the final horn, there was a full-scale melee involving players, fans, and other assorted pugilists." Whitten concedes that he isn't sure he delivered the first shot, but he may have.

Beamer rushed onto the field to act as a peacemaker. As the coach recalled it, Whitten had a Virginia player in his grasp and in his aim, and, "just as I get there, he draws back and his elbow gets my tooth." "I felt somebody jump on my back," Whitten remembered. "I assumed it was a player or a fan. I turned around, looked down, and there was Coach Beamer on the ground." A

Virginia assistant coach remarked, "Look what you've done to your coach" as though Whitten had injured Beamer intentionally. He joined other Tech players on their hands and knees amid the melee looking for Beamer's tooth, a wild scene for which Whitten does not particularly want to be remembered.

You can control much about your inevitable funeral. You can, for instance, select a funeral home, purchase a cemetery plot, pick out your casket or a tasteful urn, designate those who will deliver your eulogy, and make other less important decisions about your send-off.

What you cannot control about your death, however, is how you will be remembered and whether your demise leaves a gaping hole in the lives of those with whom you shared your life or a pothole that's quickly paved over. What determines whether those nice words someone will say about you are heartfelt truth or pleasant fabrications? What determines whether the tears that fall at your death result from heartfelt grief or a sinus infection?

Love does. Just as Paul wrote in his first letter to the Thessalonians, the love you give away during your life decides whether or not memories of you will be precious and pleasant. Love decides how you will be remembered.

I guess it's good to be remembered for something, but I thought I had a pretty good career and played for some pretty good teams. I'd hate to be remembered as the guy who knocked out Frank Beamer's tooth.
— Jimmy Whitten

**How you will be remembered after you die
is largely determined by how much
and how deeply you love others now.**

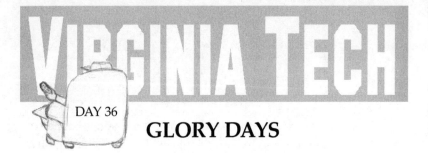

GLORY DAYS

Read Colossians 3:1-4.

"When Christ, who is your life, appears, then you also will appear with him in glory" (v. 4).

The headlines, the name in the box score, the publicity, all the glory that comes with being a star on the greatest team in Tech women's basketball history -- they didn't come Katie O'Connor's way. And yet her coach called her, "a real hero for us."

The Hokies of 1998-99 set a school record with a 28-3 record, won the Atlantic 10 championship in the regular season, advanced to the Sweet 16 in the NCAA Tournament, and enjoyed the highest national ranking in school history at No. 9. Amy Wetzel (See Devotion No. 87.) was the team's star. So what in the world was head coach Bonnie Henrickson talking about when she referred to O'Connor -- a senior forward who was only the team's fourth-leading scorer and who rarely led the team in points or rebounds in a game -- as the team's hero?

The answer lies in the fact that most of the things O'Connor did that were crucial to her team's success didn't draw attention to her. "Her number of charges taken, her great defense, the fact Katie never takes a bad shot, the fact she's a real team leader, nope, none of that ever shows up in a box score," Kenrickson said. But then she added, "That's OK, though. Everybody here knows what Katie O'Connor does for us."

Not being showered with individual glory was just fine for

O'Connor. "I'm not one of those players who is going to put up 15 or 20 points every night," she admitted. "I'm going to try and contribute eight or 10 points, try to get some boards." She contributed enough to start for four straight seasons (1995-99). And she did receive her share of the glory when she was named the conference's Most Improved Player as a senior.

But for Katie O'Connor, it was all about team glory.

You may well remember the play that was your moment of athletic glory. Or the night you received an award from a civic group for your hard work. Your first (and last?) ace on the golf course. Your promotion at work. Your first-ever 10K race. Life does have its moments of glory.

But they amount to a lesser, transient glory, which bears pain with it since you cannot recapture the moment. The excitement, the joy, even the happiness – they are fleeting; they pass as quickly as they arose, and you can never experience them again.

Glory days that last forever are found only through Jesus. That's because true glory properly belongs only to God, who has shown us his glory in Jesus. To accept Jesus into our lives is thus to take God's glory into ourselves. Glory therefore is an ongoing attribute of Christians. Our glory days are right now, and they will become even more glorious when Jesus returns.

I was brought up with the philosophy that you just do whatever you can for the team. I don't care if I score any points, as long as we win.
-- Katie O'Connor

**The glory of this earth is fleeting,
but the glory we find in Jesus lasts forever
– and will only get even more magnificent.**

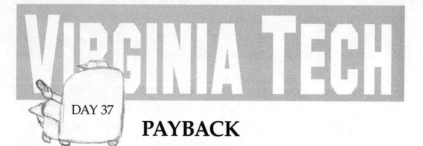

PAYBACK

Read Matthew 5:38-42.

"I tell you, Do not resist an evil person. If someone strikes you on the right cheek, turn to him the other also" (v. 39).

The newly formed Atlantic Coast Conference didn't want Virginia Tech in 1953 because its sports program was in such bad shape. The Hokies immediately proceeded to exact some revenge for the insult by whipping every ACC football team they played in 1954.

The ACC wanted to upgrade its reputation as a football league when it courted Virginia Tech in 2003, seeking to lure the Hokies away from the Big East. Tech officially joined the league on July 1, 2004. But fifty years before, Tech officials were the ones doing the courting, and they were solidly rebuffed.

Seven Southern Conference schools broke away to form the ACC in 1953; Virginia joined the new league in 1954. Tech athletic director and head football coach Frank Moseley saw clearly that except for West Virginia and the Hokies, the Southern Conference would be a league of lower-rung football programs. He therefore actively campaigned for Tech's admission to the new league -- for fifteen years. Tech never got in.

Herbert "Mac" McEver, Tech's head football coach from 1942-45, said Tech was excluded because the school's sports programs had become too weak for serious consideration. After all, the Hokies had compiled a miserable 17-54-6 record over the last eight foot-

ball seasons. By the time Moseley had rebuilt the program, ACC members decided they liked their exclusive club the way it was.

So in 1954, Moseley's Hokies exacted revenge by embarrassing the new league. The football program that wasn't good enough went 4-0 against ACC competition, whipping NC State 30-21, Wake Forest 32-0, Clemson 18-7, and Virginia 6-0.

The very nature of an intense rivalry in football is that the loser will seek payback for the defeat of the season before. But what about in life when somebody's done you wrong; is it time to get even? The problem with revenge in real-life is that it isn't as clear-cut as a scoreboard. Life is so messy that any attempt at revenge is often inadequate or, worse, backfires and injures you.

As a result, you remain gripped by resentment and anger, which hurts you and no one else. You poison your own happiness while that other person goes blithely about her business. The only way someone who has hurt you can keep hurting you is if you're a willing participant.

But it doesn't have to be that way. Jesus ushered in a new way of living when he taught that we are not to seek revenge for personal wrongs and injuries. Let it go and go on with your life. What a relief!

The first thing you know, Tech will win the Atlantic Coast Conference championship.
-- ACC Commissioner Jim Weaver before the Clemson game in 1954

Resentment and anger over a wrong injures you,
not the other person, so forget it
-- just as Jesus taught.

DAY 38

COMEBACK KID

Read Acts 9:1-22.

*"All those who heard him were astonished and asked,
'Isn't he the man who raised havoc in Jerusalem among
those who call on this name?'" (v. 21)*

Ernest Wilford used the biggest disappointment of his athletic life to make a comeback that propelled him to Hokie greatness.

On Dec. 1, 2001, the Miami Hurricanes came to Blacksburg undefeated and thinking national championship. They led 26-10 midway through the fourth quarter when the Hokies launched a comeback. Fullback Jarrett Ferguson scored from one yard out with 8:33 to play. Grant Noel hit wide receiver Terrell Parham for the two-point conversion to make it a 26-18 game.

When Miami went three-and-out, Eric Green blocked the punt, and Brandon Manning picked it up and ran 22 yards for a touchdown. With 6:03 the play, Tech trailed 26-24. On the two-point conversion attempt for the tie, Noel had plenty of time to scan the field and spotted sophomore Wilford, who had just ten catches on the season, alone in the right corner of the end zone. Noel tossed a strike, an easy catch. "[The pass] came at me like it was in slow motion," Wilford recalled. "I was debating how to catch the ball." But he didn't catch it at all; he dropped it." Tech lost 26-24.

Wilford was devastated, though his teammates didn't blame him for the loss. "That was one play," Noel said. Wilford's gaffe was so widely publicized that when director Spike Lee made an

appearance on campus later that school year he callously called Wilford out as "the guy who dropped that pass."

Wilford made a promise to himself: He would do whatever it took for him to recover from his disappointment and become the best receiver he could be. What he became was the greatest receiver in Tech history, setting a school record with 126 receptions. He completed his comeback by being named first-team All-ACC as a senior in 2003.

Life will have its setbacks whether they result from personal failures or from forces and people beyond your control. Being a Christian and a faithful follower of Jesus Christ doesn't insulate you from getting into deep trouble.

Maybe financial problems suffocated you. A serious illness put you on the sidelines. Or your family was hit with a great tragedy. Life is a series of victories and defeats. Winning isn't about avoiding defeat; it's about getting back up to compete again. It's about making a comeback of your own.

When you avail yourself of God's grace and God's power, your comeback is always greater than your setback. You are never too far behind, and it's never too late in life's game for Jesus to lead you to victory, to turn trouble into triumph. As it was with Ernest Wilford and with Paul, it's not how you start that counts; it's how you finish.

I wasn't going to let it beat me. No way.
-- Ernest Wilford on the dropped pass against Miami

**In life, victory is truly a matter of how you finish
and whether you finish with Jesus at your side.**

DAY 39

LIVE ACTION

Read James 2:14-26.

"Faith by itself, if it is not accompanied by action, is dead"
(v. 17).

While the Boston College Eagles did the talking, the Virginia Tech Hokies did the playing. The result was a good old-fashioned backside kicking in the 2008 ACC championship game.

The 18th-ranked Eagles were favored and talking big the week of the Dec. 6 game. Some players asserted they "were tougher than everybody," thus less than subtly hinting that the 8-4 Hokies were soft. With a defense that had given up only 57 yards per game to its last five foes, the Eagles bragged that nobody could run on them. But then they had to quit talking and start playing. When the dust cleared, the Hokies had thoroughly whipped them 30-12 for their second straight ACC title.

Star Tech cornerback Macho Harris took all the pregame talk seriously. "Not one time can I remember anybody calling us soft," he said, "but we came out here with a chip on our shoulder and we got the job done." Even the Hokie coaches heard the talking. "They mentioned during the week that they were tougher than everybody," associate head coach Billy Hite said. "I think they were talking about us, in particular." Senior center Ryan Shuman likewise didn't like what the Eagles had to say. "We ran it right down their throats," he pointed out in the post-game celebration.

That the Hokies did. They rushed for 150 yards, 114 of which

came from tailback Darren Evans, matching the season-high rushing total allowed by the Eagles. The Tech offense "lined up, manned up," and hogged the ball for nearly 36 minutes. Two early drives of 61 and 51 yards gave the Hokies a quick 14-0 lead.

BC closed to 14-7 in the third quarter, but Tech responded with 10 third-quarter points and coasted home. Cornerback Stephan Virgil's interception with 1:17 left in the quarter set up a 10-yard TD run by Evans that made it 24-7 and ended any Eagle talking.

For the Hokies, it was all about a little less talk and a lot more action -- and their third ACC title.

Talk is cheap. Consider your neighbor or coworker who talks without saying anything, who makes promises she doesn't keep, who brags about his own exploits, who can always tell you how to do something but never shows up for the work.

How often have you fidgeted through a meeting, impatient to get on with the work everybody is talking about doing? You know – just as the BC Eagles found out from the Hokies -- that speech without action just doesn't cut it.

That principle applies in the life of a person of faith too. Merely declaring our faith isn't enough, however sincere we may be. It is putting our faith into action that shouts to the world of the depth of our commitment to Christ. Just as Jesus' ministry was a virtual whirlwind of activity, so are we to change the world by doing.

Jesus Christ is alive; so should our faith in Him be.

Don't talk too much or too soon.

-- *Bear Bryant*

Faith that does not reveal itself in action is dead.

DAY 40

AMAZING!

Read: Luke 4:31-36.

"All the people were amazed and said to each other, 'What is this teaching? With authority and power he gives orders to evil spirits and they come out!'" (v. 36)

On a winter's night in Tallahassee, Fla., Hokie Les Henson hit what is still the most amazing shot in basketball history.

Henson, a 6-6 forward, played for Coach Charlie Moir from 1976-80, "one of the hidden stars on a series of very good Tech basketball teams." He was overshadowed by teammates such as Duke Thorpe, Wayne Robinson, and Dale Solomon, but on the night of Jan. 21, 1980, he achieved Tech basketball immortality.

That evening Tech met FSU in a Metro Conference game. The 1979-80 team would finish 21-8 and would advance to the second round of the NCAA Tournament before losing to Indiana. In Tallahassee, the game was tight all the way and was tied at 77 when FSU missed a shot with about five seconds left and Henson chased the ball down in the corner.

Teammate Dexter Reid was at halfcourt, yelling at Henson to get the ball to him for a desperate heave. "I knew we didn't have time for that," Henson said. What he did instead made basketball history. "I just turned around and threw it," he said. "Then everything seemed to slow down." Painstakingly, the ball sailed 89 feet 3 inches as the crowd went silent. Henson thought it would hit a flag hanging from the rafters, but it didn't. That's when he thought,

"That thing has a chance." It hit nothing but net, no backboard, nothing. Clean. Swish. The longest shot in basketball history.

Henson turned around to the first person he saw and said, "Can you believe that?" Nobody could. It was amazing.

The word *amazing* defines the limits of what you believe to be plausible or usual. The Grand Canyon, the birth of your children, a last-second full-court heave that wins a basketball game, those bone-crunching Hokie defensive plays -- they're amazing! You've never seen anything like that before!

Some people in Galilee felt the same way when they encountered Jesus. Jesus amazed them with the authority of his teaching, and he wowed them with his power over spirit beings. People everywhere just couldn't quit talking about him.

It would have been amazing had they not been amazed. They were, after all, witnesses to the most amazing spectacle in the history of the world: God himself was right there among them walking, talking, teaching, preaching, and healing.

Their amazement should be a part of your life too because Jesus still lives. The almighty and omnipotent God of the universe seeks to spend time with you every day – because he loves you. Amazing!

It's amazing. Some of the greatest characteristics of being a winning football player are the same ones it takes to be a Christian man.
-- Bobby Bowden

Everything about God is amazing,
but perhaps most amazing of all
is that he loves us and desires our company.

DAY 41

THE GRUDGE

Read Matthew 6:7-15.

"If you forgive men when they sin against you, your heavenly Father will also forgive you. But if you do not forgive men their sins, your Father will not forgive your sins" (vv. 14-15).

For one full football season, Hokie Bob Griffith held a grudge and planned his revenge. He ultimately, though, wound up getting his own payback from a totally unexpected source.

Griffith started 31 straight games on the offensive line from 1965-67. He was co-captain with defensive back Frank Loria on the 7-3 team of 1967. Late in the 1966 West Virginia game, Griffith blocked a Mountaineer player, who spit in his face. "I wanted to jump up and punch him, but I knew if I did, that it would take us out of field goal range," Griffith said, "so I didn't do anything."

But he didn't forget either. When the two teams played in 1967, Griffith was ready to exact his revenge. The same player gave a fair-catch signal on a punt return and then jogged away from the ball. "I came from about 50 yards away and hit him right under the chin," Griffith recalled. "The whistle hadn't blown; it was a clean hit."

There remained another chapter in the story, however. Against FSU two weeks later, an injury required that Griffith move from guard to tackle. The first time the Hokies punted, Griffith headed downfield to cover the kick. "I got hit a bunch of times," he said,

"and they were still hitting me out of bounds." After the play, Griffith trotted to the sideline and told the coaches, "Man, these tackles catch it on punt returns. I'm going back to guard."

Only years later did Griffith learn that FSU had inserted a special punt return just to hit him repeatedly after the Noles watched films of the West Virginia game and determined that Griffith's hit had been a cheap shot. The lineman's grudge had repercussions he hadn't expected.

It's probably pretty easy for you to recall times when somebody did you wrong. Have you held insistently onto your grudges so that the memory of each injury still drives up your blood pressure? Or have you forgiven that other person for what he or she did to you and shrugged it off as a lesson learned?

Jesus said to forgive others, which is exactly the sort of thing he would say. Extending forgiveness, though, is monumentally easier said than done. But here's the interesting part: You are to forgive for your sake, not for the one who injured you. When you forgive, the damage is over and done with. You can move on with your life, leaving the pain behind. The past – and that person -- no longer has power over you.

Holding a grudge is a way to self-destruction. Forgiving and forgetting is a way of life – a godly life.

Don't waste any time carrying around a load of bitterness. It only sours your life, and the world won't pay any attention anyway.
-- Former head coach Pat Dye

Forgiving others frees you from your past,
turning you loose to get on with your life.

DAY 42

WHO, ME?

Read Judges 6:11-23.

"'But Lord,' Gideon asked, 'how can I save Israel? My clan is the weakest in Manasseh, and I am the least in my family'" (v. 15).

As the incredible 1999 Virginia Tech football season rolled on, quarterback Michael Vick didn't have a Web site promoting him for the Heisman Trophy. The team's record-setting kicker, Shayne Graham, didn't make *Sports Illustrated*'s list of the country's ten best special teams players. But Caleb Hurd had such a Web site and made that list. Who?

Hurd's reaction to his surprising fame was a bemused, "Who, me?" That's because he specialized in what may well be the most obscure job in college football: He was Graham's holder on kicks.

Hurd's journey from obscurity to fame started in Tech's third game of the '99 season, a 31-11 romp past Clemson. During the game, an ESPN camera showed some fans with a sign that read, "Caleb Hurd for Heisman." It was a bunch of sixth-year graduate students who thought it would be fun to root for the holder.

The following week, Hurd received an e-mail from the students asking for his permission to launch a Web site pitching him for the Heisman. Hurd went along with the fun and consented. Graham, who is Hurd's second cousin, did his part, urging Hurd to strike a Heisman pose after a field goal. Hurd's campaign fell just a wee bit short. Vick came in third; Hurd didn't get a single vote.

But Hurd went national when, in late November, *Sports Illustrated* named him among the nation's best special teams players, which was probably true. In the first game of his Tech career, the 1996 opener against Akron, Hurd bobbled the snap on a wet field. That was the only one; more than 260 placement snaps later, Hurd's soft hands were still catching every ball. "It's pretty incredible when you think about it," Frank Beamer once said.

You probably know exactly how Caleb Hurd felt when he was suddenly singled out, though perhaps you didn't enjoy it as much as he did. You know that "Who, Me?" feeling. How about that time the teacher called on you when you hadn't done a lick of homework? Or the night the hypnotist pulled you out of a room full of folks to be his guinea pig? You've had the wide-eyed look and the turmoil in your midsection when the spotlight suddenly turned on you, and placed you in a situation you neither sought nor were prepared for.

You may feel the same way Gideon did about being called to serve God in some way, quailing at the very thought of being audacious enough to teach Sunday school, lead a small group study, or coordinate a high school prayer club. After all, who's worthy enough to do anything like that?

The truth is that nobody is – but that doesn't seem to matter to God. And it's his opinion, not yours, that counts.

That's a thing I really don't understand.
-- Caleb Hurd on his unprecedented fame

You're right in that no one is worthy to serve God,
but the problem is that doesn't matter to God.

DAY 43

THE ANSWER

Read Colossians 2:2-10.

*"My purpose is that they . . . may know the mystery of
God, namely, Christ, in whom are hidden all the treasures
of wisdom and knowledge" (vv. 2, 3).*

Tech's new soccer head coach had a whole bunch of problems on
his hand; he needed some answers and he needed them quickly.
He found them in Germany.

In the spring of 2002, Oliver Weiss took over the Tech men's
soccer program. The recruiting season had passed and the new
one was months away. The school had not signed a single new
recruit because of administrative orders to wait on the new head
honcho. The team had lost five starters to graduation.

But, Weiss knew where to find the answers. "I was late getting
started," he said. "So what do you do? Try to inject an adrenaline
shot and go abroad where perhaps you can find someone."

Weiss went back home to his native Germany. There he found
Lasse Mertins in Rotenburg and Peer Rogge in Schleswig. (The
success in recruiting Mertins would reap further dividends for
Weiss when Alexander Baden, also of Rotenburg, came to Tech.
Baden was a co-captain as a senior in 2009.)

Weiss' two imports started every game in 2002 and gave the
Hokies "the boost they needed." Midfielder Mertins was twice
the Big East Rookie of the Week. Rogge, a freshman midfielder,
was once named the Rookie of the Week. They were key compo-

nents of the 2003 team, which made Tech's first-ever appearance in the NCAA Tournament.

Mertins was an Academic All-America and second-team All-Big East in 2003. Rogge was third-team All-Big East that season. Together, they provided some of the answers needed to propel Tech soccer into the big time.

Experience is essentially the uncovering of answers to some of life's questions, both trivial and profound. You often discover that as soon as you learn a few answers, the questions change. Your children get older, your health worsens, your financial situation changes, one of Tech's teams struggles unexpectedly -- all situations requiring answers to a new set of difficulties.

No answers, though, are more important than the ones you seek in your search for God and the meaning of life because they determine your fate for all eternity. Since a life of faith is a journey and not a destination, the questions do indeed change with your circumstances. The "why" or the "what" you ask God when you're a teenager is vastly different from the quandaries you ponder as an adult.

No matter how you phrase the question, though, the answer inevitably centers on Jesus. And that answer never changes.

When you're a driver and you're struggling in the car, you're looking for God to come out of the sky and give you a magical answer.
-- NASCAR's Rusty Wallace

It doesn't matter what the question is;
if it has to do with life, temporal or eternal,
the answer lies in Jesus.

CHANCE MEETING

Read Luke 24:13-35.

*"That same day two of them were going to a village. . . .
They were talking with each other about everything that
had happened. . . . Jesus himself came up and walked
along with them" (vv. 13-15).*

A chance meeting and a casual conversation that he wasn't
even a part of resulted in an ag major from England who came to
America to milk cows being the Hokie football team's kicker.

Jon Utin grew up in Oxford, England, and literally came to the
U.S.A. to milk cows. He was a dairy science major whose college
required that he spend a year on a farm, and he wound up on a
dairy farm in Virginia. One day at an agricultural meeting, Utin
had a chance encounter with a Tech man who suggested he come
to Blacksburg and get a degree in dairy science. Utin liked the idea
and ultimately went to Tech on a Sears & Roebuck scholarship,
leading head coach Jerry Claiborne to quip once that Utin was the
best thing he'd ever gotten out of a Sears & Roebuck catalog.

At Tech, Utin studied, ran track, and played soccer -- until yet
another chance encounter changed his life again. John Ghee, a
Tech soccer player, was casually talking football one day with
a graduate assistant coach who remarked that the team might
be pretty good if it could find a kicker. "You know," said Ghee,
"there's a guy on the soccer team from England who can kick
really well." That guy, of course, was Utin. As a result, Clairborne

invited Utin to practice the last week of the 1964 season.

"I really had no clue what was going on," Utin said, which was true because he had seen only one Tech football game in his life. He kicked a few times at that practice, later found a book by legendary kicker Lou Groza and studied it, put what he read there into practice, and won the starting place-kicking job in the fall of '65. He was the Hokie kicker for three seasons.

Maybe you met your spouse on a blind date or in Kroger's frozen food section. Perhaps a conversation in an elevator or over lunch led to a job offer.

Chance meetings often shape our lives. Some meetings, however, are too important to be left to what seem like the whims of life. If your child is sick, you don't wait until you happen to bump into a physician at Starbuck's to seek help.

So it is with Jesus. Too much is at stake to leave a meeting with him to chance. Instead, you intentionally seek him at church, in the pages of your Bible, on your knees in prayer, or through a conversation with a friend or neighbor. How you conduct the search doesn't matter; what matters is that you find him.

Once you've met him, you should then intentionally cultivate the acquaintance until it is a deep, abiding, life-shaping and life-changing friendship.

It was a strange door that brought me to this country, and several other strange doors opened for me, like the one that brought me to Tech.
-- Jon Utin

A meeting with Jesus should not be a chance encounter, but instead should be sought out.

CASH AND CARRY

Read 1 Peter 1:13-25.

"It was not with perishable things such as silver or gold that you were redeemed from the empty way of life handed down to you from your forefathers, but with the precious blood of Christ" (vv. 18-19).

On a night that ended with joyous Hokies chucking oranges into the stands, quarterback Sean Glennon in particular and his teammates in general found redemption.

On Dec. 1, 2007, sixth-ranked Tech met 12th-ranked Boston College in Jacksonville, Fla., in the ACC Championship Game. Very much on the mind of the Tech players was a last-second 14-10 loss to the Eagles back on Oct. 25. "We wanted to get back at them," senior flanker Eddie Royal admitted. "They spoiled our national championship hopes and we wanted to take this game." The Hokies did take the game and a berth in the Orange Bowl, pummeling the Eagles 30-16.

But the night was about more than just sweet redemption for a team. It was also about redemption for Glennon, the junior quarterback who at one time during the season was relegated to the bench for poor play and was apparently done for the season.

After the Hokies lost to LSU on Sept. 8, Glennon was benched in favor of freshman Tyrod Taylor. He stayed on the sideline until Oct. 13 when Taylor was injured in the Duke game. Glennon then stepped in and played so well while Taylor was out that head

coach Frank Beamer decided to go to a two-man rotation when Taylor returned.

In the championship game, Glennon was 18-for-27 passing for 174 yards and three touchdowns. He was named the MVP. This was "a redemption thing for Sean, too," Royal said after the game as Glennon clutched an orange in one hand and his MVP trophy in the other. The redemption provided him by the game, Glennon said, "shows how blessed I've been."

In our capitalistic society, we know all about redemption. Just think "rebate" or store or product coupons. To receive the rebates or the discount, though, we must redeem them, cash them in.

"Redemption" is a business term; it reconciles a debt, restoring one party to favor by making amends. In the Bible, a slave could obtain his freedom only by a redeemer's paying money. In other words, redemption involves the cancelling of a debt the individual cannot pay on his own.

While literal, physical slavery is incomprehensible to us today, we nevertheless live much like slaves in our relationship to sin. On our own, we cannot escape from its consequence: death. We need a redeemer, someone to pay the debt that then gives us the forgiveness from sin we cannot give ourselves. We have such a redeemer. He is Jesus Christ, who paid our debt not with money, but with his own blood.

Redemption. That's all we were thinking about this week.
-- Eddie Royal before the 2007 championship game

To accept Jesus Christ as your savior is to believe
his death was a selfless act of redemption.

DAY 46

CALLING IT QUITS

Read Numbers 13:25-14:4.

"The men who had gone up with him said, 'We can't attack those people; they are stronger than we are'" (v. 13:31).

A player who had quit and was throwing up every day at practice and a coach who impressed him with his toughness kept tackle Ron Frank from twice quitting the Hokie football team.

Frank started for Tech both in 1962 and in 1963, the latter squad the Southern Conference champions and the only Virginia Tech team to win that league title outright. As a sophomore in 1961, he played both ways for the first two games, but then was benched during the third game. "They never talked to me about it, so I don't know what took place," Frank said. He didn't play another down that season and said, "I couldn't quite figure that out."

He came back in 1962, but before the season began, he decided to quit, even calling his parents to tell them. They tried to talk him into staying, but Frank was on schedule to graduate and figured he could pay for his education for one year himself. So he told head coach Jerry Claiborne he was quitting.

But Bloice Davison, who had quit the Tech team the year before, intervened. He had returned to the squad and, according to Frank, "was back out there playing without a scholarship and puking every day." He advised Frank not to quit, and Frank listened.

When Frank graduated in June 1963, he considered not coming

back for what would be his senior season. But he recalled an incident in the fall of 1962 when Claiborne was coaching from a golf cart because he had had back surgery. On the sideline during a game, Claiborne was knocked down by an opposing player. When an assistant tried to help him up, Claiborne barked, "I'll get up myself." As Frank watched, the coach bit down on his cane to avoid groaning in pain and got up. Frank told himself, "If he's tough enough to do that, I'm tough enough to come back for another year." He came back for the championship season.

Remember that time you quit a high-school sports team? Bailed out of a relationship? Walked away from that job with the goals unachieved? Sometimes quitting is the most sensible way to minimize your losses, so you may well at times in your life give up on something or someone.

In your relationship with God, however, you should remember the people of Israel, who quit when the Promised Land was theirs for the taking. They forgot one fact of life you never should: God never gives up on you.

That means you should never, ever give up on God. No matter how tired or discouraged you get, no matter that it seems your prayers aren't getting through to God, no matter what – quitting on God is not an option. He is preparing a blessing for you, and in his time, he will bring it to fruition -- if you don't quit on him.

If you quit now, next time the going gets tough, you'll quit again.
– Bloice Davison to Ron Frank

Whatever else you give up on in your life, don't give up on God; he will never ever give up on you.

BLESS YOU

Read Romans 5:1-11.

"We also rejoice in our sufferings because we know that suffering produces perseverance; perseverance, character; and character, hope. And hope does not disappoint us" (vv. 3-5a).

God's greatest blessings sometimes appear to be anything but providential, a faith lesson that Hokie second baseman Marc Tugwell learned while he was at Tech.

A four-year starter for the Hokies, Tugwell hit .398 as a senior in 2003. He was honorable mention All-America, first team All-Big East, and the league's Co-Player of the Year. He set the Virginia Tech career records for putouts and assists by a second baseman. As a junior in 2002, he hit .342 and was first-team All-Big East.

In the fall of 2001, however, Tugwell made what he called a "stupid" mistake and was suspended from school for the fall 2002 semester. That sent him into involuntary exile at home and a job in a Mexican restaurant. Tugwell's father was quick to notice that what was clearly not the highlight of his son's life was actually "a blessing in disguise. He saw from a different perspective what it's going to be like [as a working adult]," Tugwell's dad said about the suspension. "He had to get up every day, put on a tie, which probably helped motivate him a little bit, too."

He was motivated enough to spend more than two hours a day for three days each week at a local gym, paying for it himself.

The result is that Tugwell returned to school faster and stronger. He put on about ten pounds, decreased his time in the 60-yard dash, and improved his ability to hit for power. Tugwell led the team in 2003 in batting, homers, hits, runs, and both on-base and slugging percentage. His time of trial turned into a blessing that transformed him into a much better baseball player.

"You learn your lesson," Tugwell said of the suspension. "It was a blessing in disguise."

Quite often, we don't know exactly what God is up to in our lives. We can know, though, that he's always busy preparing blessings for us and that if we trust and obey him, he will pour out those blessings upon us.

Some of those blessings, however, come disguised as hardship and suffering as was the case with Marc Tugwell. That's often true in our own lives, too, and it is only after we can look back upon what we have endured that we understand it as a blessing.

The key lies in trusting God, in realizing that God isn't out to destroy us, but instead is interested only in doing good for us, even if that means allowing us to endure the consequences of a difficult lesson. God doesn't manage a candy store; more often, he relates to us as a stern but always loving father. If we truly love and trust God, no matter what our situation is now, he has blessings in store for us. This, above all, is our greatest hope.

If there's such a thing as a blessing in disguise, that was one.
-- Tech baseball coach Chuck Hartman on Marc Tugwell's suspension

**Life's hardships are often transformed into
blessings when we endure them trusting in God.**

DAY 48

TOLD YOU SO

Read Matthew 24:15-31.

"See, I have told you ahead of time" (v. 25).

Trotting off the field, Frank Peake just couldn't resist telling his coach, "I told you so."

Peake was an integral part of the legendary "Pony Express," the backfield that came to Blacksburg in 1925 as part of the first Tech class to receive football scholarships. Herbert "Mac" McEver, Tommy Tomko, and Scotty MacArthur completed the Express.

A "fleet back who loved the open field," Peake would have an All-American career at Tech. He was inducted into the Virginia Sports Hall of Fame in 1978 and the Virginia Tech Sports Hall of Fame in 1983 in its second class.

As a senior in 1928, Peake suffered a hip injury against Maryland, a week before the showdown with Virginia. The injury was severe enough to land him in the Tech infirmary for five days. He talked his doctor into letting him attend the game, only after receiving strict instructions not to play. In the locker room, Peake also managed to talk head coach Andy Gustafson into letting him suit up so he could sit on the bench with the team.

On a cold, snowy day, Virginia drove into Tech territory four times in the first half but couldn't score while halfback Phil Spear scored a second-quarter touchdown for the Hokies. Just before the half, Tech drove to the Virginia 11 but stalled. Peake then began to beg Gustafson to let him run it. The coach relented, and

Peake quickly scored.

In the third quarter, Peake was at it again, begging his coach for the chance to return a punt. He clinched his argument by promising, "They won't touch me." He then fielded the punt and "twisted and side-stepped his way" to a 70-yard touchdown. "See," Peake said as he came back to the bench. "I told you they wouldn't touch me." Tech won 20-0.

Don't you just hate it in when somebody says, "I told you so"? That means the other person was right and you were wrong; that other person has spoken the truth. You could have listened to that know-it-all in the first place, but then you would have lost the chance yourself to crow, "I told you so."

In our pluralistic age and society, many view truth as relative, meaning absolute truth does not exist. All belief systems have equal value and merit. But this is a ghastly, dangerous fallacy because it ignores the truth that God proclaimed in the presence and words of Jesus.

In speaking the truth, Jesus told everybody exactly what he was going to do: come back and take his faithful followers with him. Those who don't listen or who don't believe will be left behind with those four awful words, "I told you so," ringing in their ears and wringing their souls.

There's nothing in this world more instinctively abhorrent to me than finding myself in agreement with my fellow humans.
-- Lou Holtz

Jesus matter-of-factly told us what he has planned:
He will return to gather all the faithful to himself.

THE INTERVIEW

Read Romans 14: 1-12.

"We will all stand before God's judgment seat. . . . So then, each of us will give an account of himself to God"
(vv. 10, 12).

Tech head coach Bill Dooley once conducted a postgame, locker-room interview while he stood barefoot in water.

In the late 1970s and early 1980s, Virginia Tech underwent what writer Chris Colston called "an identity crisis." Today, the notion that Virginia Tech would not be a major player in college sports is ludicrous. But as Dooley was hired in 1978, many on campus felt strongly that academics should be the priority; others conceded that point but argued that Tech's untapped athletic potential should be loosed upon unsuspecting collegiate opponents.

Dooley's hire seem to declare that Tech was committed to big-time football. The schedule said otherwise, however, as Dooley found himself playing the old standbys such as VMI, William & Mary, and Richmond. "Are we really stepping up, or was Bill Dooley coming here just to win games against mediocre competition?" asked Jeff Charles, the former voice of the Hokies.

As the "tug of war" raged, Dooley and his coaches often had to improvise under less than ideal circumstances. For instance, the weather was cold for the Virginia game Thanksgiving night 1982. Short of warm weather gear, offensive coordinator Pat Watson sent equipment manager Lester Karlin to KMart to buy every pair

of queen-sized pantyhose and all the work gloves he could find. And then there was the infamous interview in the water, which in fact ended the Oyster Bowl, a biennual game against VMI at Norfolk's Foreman Field. After the 54-7 Hokies win, the old facility's plumbing failed, and nearly six inches of water filled the Tech locker room. Dooley answered media questions "at the door of the locker room, in his bare feet, water above his ankles, as the reporters stood outside."

You may well never be the subject of a reporter's interview, but you probably know about interviews of another kind: the dreaded job interview. You've experienced the stress and the anxiety as you tried to appear somewhat composed while coming up with reasonably original answers to banal questions and hiding your conviction that the interviewer was a total geek. You told yourself that if they turned you down, it was their loss, not yours.

You won't be so indifferent, though, about your last interview: the one with God. A day will come when we will all stand before God to account for ourselves. It is to God and God alone – not our friends, not our parents, not society in general – that we must give a final and complete account. Since all eternity will be at stake, it sure would help to have a surefire reference with you. One – and only one -- is available: Jesus Christ.

I don't think that we will be returning to the Oyster Bowl.
-- Bill Dooley during his waterlogged 1984 interview with reporters

**You will have one last interview -- with God --
and you sure want Jesus there with you
as a character witness.**

LANGUAGE BARRIER

Read Mark 16:9-20.

"Go into all the world and preach the good news to all creation" (vv. 3-4 NRSV).

One of Tech's greatest women's basketball players was so unsure of her English that she would communicate only by e-mail when she was recruited and waited until her junior year in Blacksburg to take freshman English because she was petrified she wouldn't pass.

Ieva Kublina was a 6-4 forward for the Tech women from 2000-2004. She was first-team All-Big East as a junior and second team as a senior. She is the third leading scorer in Tech history with 1,647 points, set the school career record for blocked shots with 256, and is second in career rebounding with 845. In 2003, she was the Virginia Tech Female Athlete of the Year.

Kublina grew up in Latvia where she was spotted by a coach from Virginia Commonwealth playing in a European tournament. He encouraged her to come to America as a high school exchange student. Her close-knit family was so reluctant to have her leave home that they needed six months to make the decision.

Kublina could read and write English well enough, but speaking it was another matter. When Tech coach Bonnie Henrickson recruited her, Kublina would use only e-mails. At Tech, she had to take a crash course in both college basketball and its lingo. When the coaches noticed a puzzled look on her face, they would repeat

the instructions so as not to embarrass her.

The language problems gradually disappeared, and Kublina morphed from a shy foreigner into what her roommate described as a "very sarcastic, very funny" college student. And that freshman English course? Like her other class work -- no problem.

As Ieva Kublina's experience demonstrates, our games often translate across national and cultural boundaries while it is our language that usually erects a barrier to understanding. Recall your overseas vacation or your call to a tech support number when you got someone who spoke English but didn't understand it. Talking loud and waving your hands doesn't facilitate communication; it just makes you look weird.

Like many other aspects of life, faith has its jargon that can sometimes hinder understanding. Sanctification, justification, salvation, Advent, Communion with its symbolism of eating flesh and drinking blood – these and many other words have specific meanings to Christians that may be incomprehensible, confusing, and downright daunting to the newcomer or the seeker.

But the heart of Christianity's message centers on words that require no explanation: words such as hope, joy, love, purpose, and community. Their meanings are universal because people the world over seek them in their lives. Nobody speaks that language better than Jesus.

Kindness is the universal language that all people understand.
-- Legendary Florida A&M Coach Jake Gaither

Jesus speaks across all language barriers
because his message of hope and meaning
resounds with people everywhere.

TEN TO REMEMBER

Read Exodus 20:1-17.

"God spoke all these words: 'I am the Lord your God . . . .
You shall have no other gods before me'" (vv. 1, 3).

Shayne Graham's last-play, game-winning field goal that beat West Virginia. (See Devotion No. 22.) That was one writer's pick for the top play of the incredible 1999 Hokie football season.

The day Tech whipped Boston College 38-14 to complete an undefeated season, Randy King of *The Roanoke Times* named his "Top 10 Moments of the Season." Topping his list was Graham's 44-yard kick that propelled Tech to a 22-20 win and an 8-0 record.

No. 2 on the list occurred right before Graham's kick: quarterback Michael Vick's 26-yard sideline scramble that carried the Hokies to the WVa 36. Defensive end Corey Moore's "monster" game in Tech's 31-11 win over Clemson was King's No. 3. Moore had five tackles, two sacks, and two more tackles for loss; he also forced a fumble and broke up a pass.

No. 4 was Vick's acrobatic 7-yard touchdown run in the 47-0 romp over James Madison. King's fifth best moment of the season was a conglomerate of the help Tech received from other teams on its way to the No. 2 national ranking. King's No. 6 best moment was the 62-0 flogging of Syracuse (See Devotion No. 8.) with ESPN's "College GameDay" crew in the house. No. 7 for this season to remember was Tech's 43-10 demolition of Miami in what was dubbed the Big East game of the year.

King's eighth best moment of the season was Vick's first-half performance in the 58-20 beatdown at Rutgers. Vick completed 11 of 12 passes for 248 and four touchdowns and ran for 68 yards and another score: 316 yards of offense and five TDs in one half.

No. 9 was Andre Kendrick's 162 yards rushing in the 30-17 win at Pittsburgh; King's tenth top play of the season was Andre Davis' 60-yard TD catch from Vick in the 31-7 win at Virginia.

For Hokies fans, these are indeed ten plays to remember.

You've got your list and you're ready to go: a gallon of paint and a water hose from the hardware store; chips, peanuts, and sodas from the grocery store for watching tonight's football game; the tickets for the band concert. Your list helps you remember.

God also made a list once of things he wanted you to remember; it's called the Ten Commandments. Just as your list reminds you to do something, so does God's list remind you of how you are to act in your dealings with other people and with him.

A life dedicated to Jesus is a life devoted to relationships, and God's list emphasizes that the social life and the spiritual life of the faithful cannot be sundered. God's relationship to you is one of unceasing, unqualified love, and you are to mirror that divine love in your relationships with others. In case you forget, you have a list.

Society today treats the Ten Commandments as if they were the ten suggestions. Never compromise on right or wrong.
-- College baseball coach Gordie Gillespie

God's list is a set of instructions on how you are to conduct yourself with other people and with him.

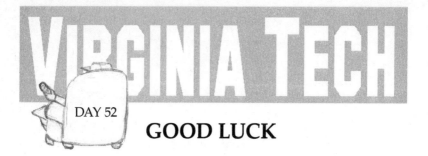

GOOD LUCK

Read 1 Samuel 28:3-20.

"Saul then said to his attendants, 'Find me a woman who is a medium, so I may go and inquire of her'" (v. 7).

The Hokies changed everything they could (except their favorite restaurant) to end the hex against Southern Mississippi. In the end, their Ace in the hole made the difference.

Coach Bill Foster's men's basketball team of 1994-95 set a Tech record with 25 wins and won the NIT. The Hokies got off to a great start and were 10-2 when they traveled to Hattiesburg to play Southern Miss on Jan. 7. Foster was keenly aware that Tech had lost eleven straight to the Eagles. The hex was worse in Hattiesburg where the Hokies had lost nine straight games and had not won since 1985.

Foster proceeded to shake up everything he could to end the hex. He changed motels for his team; he switched locker rooms. "We changed everything but restaurants," said sophomore forward Ace Custis about pre-game preparations. Why not change the restaurant? "The food was too good there," Custis explained. The motel the team abandoned "was a little better, too," Custis said, "but we were willing to try anything" to get a win.

In the end, Custis and not a different motel or locker rooms was the key to ending the longstanding hex. He scored 20 points and snared a career-high 19 rebounds to pace the exorcism of the Southern Miss demon 87-72.

In 1997, when his Tech career ended, Custis became only the third men's basketball player in school history to have his jersey retired. He joined Chris Smith and Bill Matthews as the only Tech players to score more than 1,000 points and grab more than 1,000 rebounds in their careers.

In 1995, though, he helped break the hex.

Black cats are right pretty. A medium is a steak. A key chain with a rabbit's foot wasn't too lucky for the rabbit. And what in the world is a blarney stone? About as superstitious as you get is to say "God bless you" when somebody sneezes.

You look indulgently upon good-luck charms, tarot cards, astrology, palm readers, and the like; they're really just amusing and harmless. So what's the problem? Nothing as long as you conduct yourself with the belief that superstitious objects and rituals – from broken mirrors to your daily horoscope – can't bring about good or bad luck. You aren't willing to let such notions and nonsense rule your life.

The danger of superstition lies in its ability to lure you into trusting it, thus allowing it some degree of influence over your life. In that case, it subverts God's rightful place.

Whether or not it's superstition, something does rule your life. It should be God – and God alone.

I don't think we'll ever see this place again.
-- A relieved Bill Foster after the 1995 win in Hattiesburg on the
impending break-up of the Metro Conference

Superstitions may not rule your life, but
something does; it should be God and God alone.

DAY 53

TIME FOR A CHANGE

Read Romans 6:1-14.

"Just as Christ was raised from the dead through the glory of the Father, we too may live a new life" (v. 4).

Michael Vick's life literally changed overnight.

Perhaps even before Vick realized it, Frank Beamer did. On the day after the 2000 Sugar Bowl, Beamer did a radio interview, and it wasn't at all what he expected. "Florida State had just won the national championship and all the people wanted to talk about was Michael Vick," an amazed Beamer said.

And why not? Though the Seminoles had indeed won the game and the national title, Vick had stolen the show and the spotlight. He had "dodged, darted, scrambled and escaped" for 322 yards against the nation's best defense. "On the basis of one night, [he became] the most recognizable face" in college football.

The reality of how much his life had changed hit Vick a few days after the game. He spent some time with his family and was casually headed home one evening in his nondescript 1994 Honda when a car pulled alongside his. "I looked to the side," Vick recalled, "and I could see all these people, like, pointing at me, hollering 'That's him right there.' . . . I pretty much realized that things would never ever be the same again for Michael Vick."

They never were. With his sudden celebrity came some benefits. In February, Vick went to Las Vegas where he won the ESPY for college football player of the year. He found himself hobnobbing

with some of the biggest names in sports: Tiger Woods, Peyton Manning, Jerry Rice and the like. And they knew his name

But the change also came with a down side: He lost his anonymity forever. Everywhere he went, autograph hounds swamped him. He couldn't even go to a Blacksburg grocery store without being surrounded and corralled by fans.

Michael Vick's life had changed radically forever.

Anyone who asserts no change is needed in his or her life just isn't paying attention. Every life has doubt, worry, fear, failure, frustration, unfulfilled dreams, and unsuccessful relationships in some combination. The memory and consequences of our past often haunt and trouble us.

Recognizing the need for change in our lives, though, doesn't mean the changes that will bring about hope, joy, peace, and fulfillment will occur. We need some power greater than ourselves or we wouldn't be where we are.

So where can we turn to? Where lies the hope for a changed life? It lies in an encounter with he who is the Lord of all Hope: Jesus Christ. For a life turned over to Jesus, change is inevitable. With Jesus in charge, the old self with its painful and destructive ways of thinking, feeling, loving, and living is transformed.

A changed life is always only a talk with Jesus away.

Just like that, in the time it takes to play one football game, the whole world changed for Michael Vick. If you think about it, it's crazy, man.
-- Michael Vick after the 2000 Sugar Bowl

**In Jesus lie the hope and the power
that change lives.**

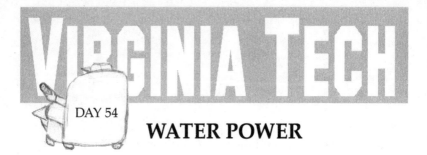

WATER POWER

Read Acts 10:34-48.

"Can anyone keep these people from being baptized with water? They have received the Holy Spirit just as we have" (v. 47).

Water was both the inspiration and the instigation behind a wild night in the Tech athletic dorm that included a water slide, the flooding of four floors, and the rescue of a drowning dog.

On a cold night in February 1967, several athletes came in late and gathered in Frank Beamer's room on the third floor of Miles Hall about 2 a.m.. One of them unwisely sat on the sink, which promptly broke away from the wall, spraying water all over the room and sending it rushing down the hallway.

Team kicker Jon Utin used pliers to turn the water off, but no one could see the sense of letting all that perfectly good water go to waste. They rounded up all the detergent and soap they could find and sprinkled it all down the hall. That created a water slide with the athletes getting a running start at one end of the hall, sitting down, and sliding all the way to the other end.

After about an hour or so, somebody mentioned the very good chance that coach Jerry Claiborne would kill them all if he found out, so they swept the water down the staircase. Which promptly flooded the second floor. They then moved the water to the first floor, which flooded it, and then to the basement, which flooded it, but at least they had the water out of sight and thus out of mind.

Until somebody remembered the dog. One of the football players had found a dog that had been hit by a car, had taken it to a vet, and was hiding it in the basement from the coaches until its broken leg healed. The panicked players scrambled downstairs to find the dog with his head just barely above water. They managed to unclog a drain, and the water obligingly went its way.

The next morning, the building custodian was delighted. He told the players he had never seen the floors so clean.

Children's wading pools and swimming pools in the backyard. Fishing, boating, skiing, and swimming at a lake. Sun, sand, and surf at the beach. If there's any water around, we'll probably be in it, on it, or near it. If there's not any at hand, we'll build a dam and create our own.

We love the wet stuff for its recreational uses, but water first and foremost is about its absolute necessity to support and maintain life. From its earliest days, the Christian church appropriated water as an image of life through the ritual of baptism. Since the time of the arrival of the Holy Spirit at Pentecost, baptism with water has been the symbol of entry into the Christian community. It is water that marks a person as belonging to Jesus. It is through water that a person proclaims that Jesus is his Lord.

There's something in the water, all right. There is life.

Let's open up all the windows and go ice skating.
— Defensive end/linebacker Doug Thacker's suggestion (thankfully rejected) about what to do with all the water on the floor of Miles Hall

There is life in the water:
physical life and spiritual life.

FAMILY TIES

Read Mark 3:31-35.

*"[Jesus] said, 'Here are my mother and my brothers!
Whoever does God's will is my brother and sister and
mother'" (vv. 34-35).*

The 1954 Virginia Tech football team is the only one in modern
times to go undefeated. The squad was loaded with talent, but it
had something more: It had family ties.

The '54 team, which went 8-0-1, "was a dream squad, the fruit
of [head coach Frank] Moseley's three years of hard recruiting.
[They] were small, swift, and smart. They were deep in talent at
the skill positions." The heart and soul of the team was its experienced seniors: ends Tom Petty and Bob Luttrell, future Baltimore
Colt tackle George Preas, guards Billy Kerfoot (the team captain)
and Jim Haren, halfbacks Billy Anderson and Howie Wright, and
quarterback John Dean. But the team also had what was called an
"unbelievable stable of underclassmen."

Center-linebacker Jack Prater, who returned to the team as a
sophomore after a two-year hitch in the army, said the team wasn't
big, but "It was the era of racehorse football, and we fit the bill. . . .
We were probably one of the fastest teams in Tech history."

The team began the season grandly with successive wins over
North Carolina State, Wake Forest, and Clemson. After a win
over Richmond came a hard-fought 6-0 defeat of Virginia. The
score came on a 20-yard pass from Billy Cranwell to sophomore

end Grover Jones. Following an inexplicable 7-7 tie with William and Mary, the team finished with three straight wins.

Tech had had teams with talent before, but this team was different because of what was termed "another, even larger, factor: chemistry." Leo Burke, who played quarterback, halfback, and fullback, said the key to the team was its closeness, "that family-type feeling, that togetherness."

The '54 Hokies weren't just a team; they were a family.

Some wit said families are like fudge, mostly sweet with a few nuts. You can probably call the names of your sweetest relatives, whom you cherish, and of the nutty ones too, whom you mostly try to avoid at a family reunion. Like it or not, you have a family, and that's God's doing. God cherishes the family so much that he chose to live in one as a son, a brother, and a cousin.

One of Jesus' more startling actions was to redefine the family. No longer is it a single household of blood relatives or even a clan or a tribe. Jesus' family is the result not of an accident of birth but rather a conscious choice. Everyone who does God's will is a member of Jesus' family.

What a startling and downright wonderful thought! You have family members out there you don't even know who stand ready to love you just because you're part of God's family.

There was never any animosity over who was getting playing time. When we went out on the field, we all went out together.
-- Leo Burke on the closeness of the 1954 Hokies

For followers of Jesus, family comes not from a shared ancestry but from a shared faith.

DAY 56

HOMELESS

Read Matthew 8:18-22.

"Jesus replied, 'Foxes have holes and birds of the air have nests, but the Son of Man has no place to lay his head'" (v. 20).

In the modern era, all Virginia Tech has ever wanted was a single home for its athletics teams." It took more than fifty years, however, to find that home.

Tech athletic director C.P. Miles was instrumental in the creation of the Southern Conference in 1921 with the Hokies among the charter members. Thirteen schools left the unwieldy league in December 1932 to form the Southeastern Conference; a second revolution in 1953 gave birth to the Atlantic Coast Conference.

When Tech didn't get into the ACC, Hokie athletic director Frank Moseley tried for fifteen years to have Tech admitted into the league; his efforts failed. Tech remained in the Southern Conference until administrators opted for independence in 1965, thus officially rendering Tech's sports programs homeless.

School president T. Marshall Hahn immediately launched a concerted effort to gain ACC membership, but was rebuffed without a formal vote. Another attempt in 1977 to join the league died after thirty minutes of discussion. Meanwhile, Hokie teams other than football played in the Metro Conference. Tech joined the Big East for football only in 1991, but efforts to find a home for all sports in the Big East were turned down in 1994.

In 1995 the Hokies and the Metro Conference underwent a messy divorce. All sports except football and wrestling moved to the Metro Conference where they remained until 2000 when Tech was granted full membership in the Big East. On July 1, 2004, more than fifty years after Frank Moseley had first tried, Tech joined the ACC. The school finally had the home it wanted for all its sports.

Rock bottom in America has a face: the bag lady pushing a shopping cart; the scruffy guy with a beard and a backpack at the interstate exit holding a cardboard sign. Look closer at that bag lady or that scruffy guy, though, and you may see desperate women with children fleeing violence, veterans haunted by their combat experiences, or sick or injured workers.

Few of us are indifferent to the homeless when we're around them. They often raise quite strong passions, whether we regard them as a ministry or a nuisance. They trouble us, perhaps because we realize that we're only one catastrophic illness and a few paychecks away from joining them. They remind us, therefore, of how tenuous our hold upon material success really is.

But they also stir our compassion because we serve a Lord who – like them -- had no home, and for whom, the homeless, too, are his children.

Virginia Tech joined the ACC after a tumultuous trek through five different conferences in the previous decade.

-- Wikipedia, the free encyclopedia.

**Because they, too, are God's children,
the homeless merit our compassion, not our scorn.**

DAY 57

FIRED UP

Read Hebrews 3:12-19.

"Exhort one another every day, as long as it is called 'today,' so that none of you may be hardened by the deceitfulness of sin" (v. 13 NRSV).

While he was a student in Blacksburg, John McCaleb was particularly bothered by a weighty matter: "Why weren't there more women at Tech?" His pondering of this imponderable led him to transform a Tech institution: the cheerleading squad.

It was 1955 when McCaleb inquired about the dearth of feminine grace and beauty on campus. The answer lay in the fact that more than a decade before, VPI had moved most of its women's programs -- and therefore its female students -- to Radford State Teachers College following the schools' merger.

The question still lay quite heavy on McCaleb's mind when he became head cheerleader of Tech's 1955-56 squad. He decided the squad needed both sprucing up and spicing up to increase school spirit; he decided it needed some females. "Getting the attention of thousands of guys sitting in the stands wasn't the easiest undertaking," McCaleb said about being a cheerleader. "But I figured if we had some gals showing their legs, well . . . ."

On-campus tryouts yielded only one cheerleader, Patsy Steckler (Bean), and McCaleb wanted four, "but there simply weren't enough women on the home campus." So he turned to Radford and was promptly swamped by 120 women trying out for the

three remaining spots. "There was a lot of crying," McCaleb remembered. He got his three cheerleaders, though: Bootie Bell (Chewning), Merle Funk, and Jeri Hagy (Justice).

McCaleb designed their uniforms himself, intentionally shaping the skirts so that when the girls spun around, "the skirt would twirl out flat and some leg would show." Cheerleading at Virginia Tech has never again been the same.

It's been a long, hard day. That couch at home is calling, but your desk is stacked with work. You're exhausted. And suddenly they show up: your personal cheerleading team. They dance, cheer, shout, wave pompoms, and generally exhort you to more and greater effort. They fire you up. That would work, wouldn't it? If only . . .

But you do have just such a squad in the most important aspect of your life: your faith. You have a big, ever growing bunch of folks who, if you will only surround yourself with them, will urge you on to a deeper, stronger relationship with Christ and to more abiding trust in God.

Who are these cheerleaders? They are your fellow believers in Christ. They come in teams -- called churches -- and they are exhorters who keep each other "in the game" that is faith. Christians are cheerleaders for God—and for God's team.

A cheerleader is a dreamer that never gives up

— Source Unknown

**In the people of your church,
you have your own set of cheerleaders
who urge you to greater faithfulness.**

DAY 58

PAIN RELIEF

Read 2 Corinthians 1:3-7.

"Just as the sufferings of Christ flow over into our lives, so also through Christ our comfort overflows" (v. 5).

Something as minor as a broken leg wasn't about to keep Billy Conaty out of the lineup for the Sugar Bowl.

Conaty is one of Virginia Tech's greatest linemen. He was a four-year letterman (1993-96) at center and was All-America as a senior. He set a school record by playing in 48 straight games.

At 6-foot-3 and 305 pounds, Conaty was a giant of a man. In the 1995 regular-season finale against Virginia, though, he was apparently felled. On the first play of the second half of the 36-29 win that capped a 9-2 season, Conaty was part of a pile of pretty serious humanity and his right leg got caught under it. "I felt it break and just snap," he said. "I was screaming bloody murder. I had never broken a bone before where I could just feel it." So what was his first thought when he knew right away he was seriously injured? "Oh, no; I'm out for the bowl game."

That certainly appeared to be the case when four days later, Conaty underwent surgery. Connected to the broken bone by seven screws, a plate was inserted into his leg for stability. But he never had any intentions of not playing in what was the biggest football game of his life. "I've played in pain before, and in a game this big, your pain tolerance goes way up," Conaty explained. "You learn to take it a little more. And it would take a whole lot to

keep me out of this one."

It wasn't just bravado. Tech needed him in the lineup and not just for his ability, as formidable as it was. He was responsible for calling the blocking assignments in the Hokies' no-huddle offense. "We need him for that reason," said offensive line coach J.B. Grimes. "He's a very pivotal guy for us."

That very pivotal guy with the broken leg was in the lineup on Dec. 31 as the Hokies rolled up 371 yards of offense and pounded Texas 28-10 in one of the biggest wins in school history.

Since you live on Earth and not in Heaven, you are forced to play with pain. Whether it's a car wreck that left you shattered, the end of a relationship that left you battered, or a loved one's death that left you tattered -- pain finds you and challenges you to keep going.

While God's word teaches that you will reap what you sow, life also teaches that pain and hardship are not necessarily the result of personal failure. Pain in fact can be one of the tools God uses to mold your character and change your life.

What are you to do when you are hit full-speed by the awful pain that seems to choke the very will to live out of you? Where is your consolation, your comfort, and your help?

In almighty God, whose love will never fail. When life knocks you to your knees, you're closer to God than ever before.

I can't let something like a little ol' broken leg keep me out.
-- Billy Conaty on playing in the Sugar Bowl

When life hits you with pain, you can always turn
to God for comfort, consolation, and hope.

DAY 59

KEEP OUT!

Read Exodus 26:31-35; 30:1-10.

"The curtain will separate the Holy Place from the Most Holy Place" (v. 26:33).

Legendary Tech center Jake Grove once got locked out of Lane Stadium -- during a game.

After being hampered by back problems for a couple of seasons, Grove moved from backup center to starting right guard in 2001. He would go on to be a unanimous All-America as a senior in 2003 and win the Dave Rimington Trophy as the nation's top center.

Grove experienced one of the most bizarre incidents in Hokie football history during the 2001 win over Central Florida. Early in the game, he suffered an injury to his left hand. A training staffer escorted him to Student Health for X-rays, which revealed his hand was broken but wouldn't keep him out of the game.

When Grove and his escort tried to return to the field, the afternoon turned surreal: They couldn't get back in. A stadium security guard told them he didn't have the key to unlock the north end-zone gate. "Here I can hear the crowd cheering and everything, and I can't get back in the place," Grove recalled. "My hand was broken and hurting me. I didn't know what to do."

One thing Grove wasn't going to do was spend the afternoon standing outside the stadium. With the trainer, he circled around the stadium to the south end, which was the site of construction for a Lane Stadium expansion. The pair managed to squeeze

through a gate only to be confronted by a steep hill. "I crawled down this dirt hill," and helped the lady trainer down, Grove said. The fans were "looking at me like, 'What is this guy doing?'"

Once at the bottom, Grove and the trainer had to crawl through a ditch. "It was a mess, a real mess," Grove said. After fifteen minutes or so of trying to get into the stadium, Grove finally made it back to the sideline.

That civic club with membership by invitation only. The bleachers where you sit while others frolic in the sky boxes. That neighborhood you can't afford a house in. You know all about being shut out of some club, some group, some place. "Exclusive" is the word that keeps you out.

The Hebrew people, too, knew about being told to keep out; only the priests could come into the presence of the holy and survive. Then along came Jesus to kick that barrier down and give us direct access to God.

In the process, though, Jesus created another exclusive club; its members are his followers, Christians, those who believe he is the Son of God and the savior of the world. This club, though, extends a membership invitation to everyone in the whole wide world; no one is excluded. Whether you're in or out depends on your response to Jesus, not on arbitrary gatekeepers.

I'm peeking over my shoulder looking for Grove on the sideline. And all along he's standing outside the stadium. It was really some crazy deal.
-- Tech offensive line coach Bryan Stinespring

Christianity is an exclusive club, but an invitation is extended to everyone and no one is denied entry.

CHEERS

Read Matthew 21:1-11.

"The crowds that went ahead of him and those that followed shouted" (v. 9).

The cheer that gave rise to Tech's famous Hokie mascot had only one slight problem: Hokie was misspelled.

In 1896, the Virginia General Assembly officially changed the school's name to the incredibly unwieldy Virginia Agricultural and Mechanical College and Polytechnic Institute. Perhaps out of dismay, citizens and fans soon shortened the name to VPI.

With the new name came a desire for new school colors -- and not a minute too soon. The original team colors of black and gray when combined with stripes led to the general opinion that the uniforms strongly resembled prison outfits. The Corps of Cadets adopted Chicago maroon and burnt orange as the official school colors, largely because no other school had that combination at the time. The new colors first appeared on Oct. 26, 1896, in a football game against Roanoke College.

The original college cheer had been "Rip! Rah! Ree! Va! Va! Vee! Virginia, Virginia, A.M.C." With the name change, it no longer applied, so a contest was held to come up with a new spirit yell. O.M. Stull, Class of 1896, created the winner (and won $5), which ultimately became known as Old Hokie. As Tech fans and alums the world over know, the cheer goes like this: "Hoki, Hoki, Hoki, Hy! Techs, Techs, VPI. Sola-Rex, Sola-Rah. Polytechs -- Virginia.

Rae, Ri, VPI." The phrase "Team! Team! Team!" was added later.

Stull said he simply made up the word "Hoki," that it had no meaning but was incorporated into the cheer because he liked the way it sounded. As it turns out, though, the word "Hokie" has been around at least since 1842 and was used to express feelings such as surprise or excitement. Thus, the word was unintentionally misspelled in the original cheer.

Chances are you go to work every day, do your job well, and then go home to your family. This country couldn't run without you; you're indispensable to the nation's efficiency. Even so, nobody cheers for you, waves pompoms in your face. or makes up a special cheer for you. Your name probably will never elicit a standing ovation when a PA announcer calls it.

It's just as well, since public opinion is notoriously fickle. Consider what happened to Jesus. When he entered Jerusalem, he was the object of raucous cheering and an impromptu parade. The crowd's adulation reached such a frenzy they tore branches off trees and threw their clothes on the ground. Five days later the crowd shouted again, screaming this time for Jesus' execution.

So don't worry too much about not having your personal set of cheering fans. Remember that you do have one personal cheerleader who will never stop pulling for you: God.

As Stull wanted, the word 'Hoki' in the popular cheer did grab attention and has been a part of Virginia Tech tradition ever since.
– 'A Look at Virginia Tech Traditions'

**Just like the sports stars, you do have
a personal cheerleader: God.**

DAY 61

ROCK SOLID

Read Luke 6:46-49.

"I will show you what he is like who comes to me and hears my words and puts them into practice. He is like a man building a house, who dug down deep and laid the foundation on rock" (vv. 47-48).

When he was thirteen years old, Bob Schweickert laid the foundation upon which he built his life.

Schweickert was Virginia Tech's starting quarterback for three seasons, 1962-64. Primarily a runner, he led the Hokies to their only outright Southern Conference championship in 1963. As a senior, the Football Writers Association named him All-America. A sprint-out, option quarterback, Schweickert was the "Mr. Outside" to running back Sonny Utz's "Mr. Inside" power running game. "He was very unselfish," Schweickert said of Utz, and "one of the best blocking backs in the country. Without Mr. Inside to keep those guys close, Mr. Outside wouldn't have had nearly the success he did."

Schweickert was such a hard worker that former head football coach Mac McEver noted, "He worked hard all the time. He didn't even walk between classes. He ran." Teammate Tommy Francisco said of Schweickert, "Any time he went to class, he carried a football with him. You'd see him going across the drill field with that football in his arms."

Schweickert grew up without a father in his life because his

dad left home when he was a youngster. Fittingly, a football stadium was the place where he found what would provide the sure and solid foundation for his life. At a Billy Graham crusade at the University of Richmond stadium when he was 13, Schweickert gave his life to the Lord. "I said this is what I want," he said. "I really accepted the Lord as my dad because I didn't have one."

You can't build anything solid and lasting unless there's a good foundation. Like Bob Schweickert's, your life is an ongoing project, a work in progress. As a complex construction job, if your life is to be stable, it must have a solid foundation, which holds everything up and keeps everything together.

R. Alan Culpepper said in *The New Interpreter's Bible,* "We do not choose whether we will face severe storms in life; we only get to choose the foundation on which we will stand." In other words, tough times are inevitable. If your foundation isn't rock-solid, you will have nothing on which to stand as those storms buffet you, nothing to keep your life from flying apart into a cycle of disappointment and destruction.

But when the foundation is solid and sure, you can take the blows, stand strong, recover, and live with joy and hope. Only one foundation is sure and foolproof: Jesus Christ. Everything else you build upon will fail you.

Virginia Tech was a part of my foundation. Jesus is the main foundation.
-- Bob Schweickert

**In the building of your life, you must start
with a foundation in Jesus Christ, or the first
trouble that shows up will knock you down.**

DAY 62

LEGAL THIEVERY

Read Exodus 22:1-15.

"A thief must certainly make restitution" (v. 2b).

The Hokies flat stole one in the Bronx.

Get the picture. On Saturday afternoon, Feb. 13, 1999, home-standing Fordham led 63-53 with 57 seconds left on the clock. "At that point," writer Randy King declared, "about the only question left was if the Hokies could shower, dress and get to LaGuardia Airport in time for a 5:20 p.m. flight home." The Fordham coach agreed. "A 10-point lead with less than a minute left," said the Rams' head man after the game. "Hey, it's in the bank." But then the Hokies pulled off nothing short of one major bank heist.

Junior guard Brendan Dunlop hit two fee throws. Senior Eddie Lucas, the team's leading scorer, intercepted the inbounds pass, was fouled, and hit two free throws. It was 63-57 with 44 seconds left. Fordham then turned the ball over nine seconds later, thanks to tight defense from senior forward Andre Ray. Tech hurried downcourt, and got a trey from reserve Jermaine Kimbrough. Suddenly, with 26.5 seconds to play, Tech trailed only 63-60.

Tech fouled immediately, and Fordham seemed to restore a little order with a free throw with 21.6 on the clock. Dunlop then drove the baseline for a layup that made it a 64-62 game with 13.4 ticks on the clock.

Another Hokie intentional foul, another Fordham free throw. But only one with 11.9 left. Dunlop, who played high school ball

nearby, then showed off for the home folks. He got his defender in the air with a ball fake, ducked under that out-of-control defender, and shot from the top of the key. "I thought [the shot] was kind of off to the left," Dunlop said. But it wasn't. Tie game. Overtime.

In the extra period, Dunlop hit two free throws for starters, and Tech never trailed again. The Hokies won 79-75, pulling off what was called "the biggest heist this side of the Brinks Robbery."

Buckle up your seat belt. Wear a bicycle or motorcycle helmet. Use your pooper scooper to clean up after your dog. Don't walk on the grass. Picky ordinances, picky laws – in all their great abundance, they're an inescapable part of our modern lives.

When Moses came stumbling down Mt. Sinai after spending time as God's secretary, he brought with him a whole mess of laws and regulations, many of which undoubtedly seem picky to us today. What some of them provide, though, are practical examples of what for God is the basic principle underlying the theft of personal property: what is wrong must be made right.

While most of us today probably won't have to worry too much about oxen, sheep, and donkeys, making what is wrong right remains a way of life for Christians. To get right with other people requires anything from restitution to apologies. To get right with God requires Jesus Christ.

When we played softball, I'd steal second base, feel guilty, and go back.
-- Woody Allen

To make right the wrong of stealing
requires restitution; to make right our
relationship with God requires Jesus Christ.

DAY 63

THE MOTHER LODE

Read John 19:25-30.

"Near the cross of Jesus stood his mother" (v. 25).

She was called "an extraordinary woman" who was hit hard in her life by heartache and suffering but who endured with "resiliency and fortitude." Fortunately for Hokie fans, she instilled those qualities in her son.

She was born with the stigma of her name attached to her like some kind of scarlet letter. Her grandfather, great uncle, a cousin, and several other family members were involved "in a spasm of violence in 1912 that left five people dead, including the judge, prosecutor and county sheriff." They shot up a Virginia courthouse and fled, an incident with its subsequent manhunt that "dominated headlines across the nation for months alongside the other huge story of that spring -- the sinking of the *Titanic*."

The incident -- and other less sensational encounters with the law -- left a scourge on the family name that she bore. "She faced obstacles every way she turned" because of her family name.

When she was 7 in 1926, her father died of pneumonia. Shortly after that, the family's farmhouse burned to the ground. "She had a tough time as a girl," summarized a relative. Neighbors and relatives helped the family rebuild, but life on a farm during the Great Depression was hard. Even as a young girl, she worked constantly just to help the family stay fed.

She grew into "a smart, pretty young woman" who used her

determination and grit to secure a teaching certificate. She fell in love, married, and gave her husband four children. Each of the pregnancies was difficult, especially the last as her labor stretched into days. As she had done throughout her life, she relied on her faith and her fortitude. She "prayed and prayed" and "told the Lord that if he would allow the child to be born she would do everything she could for the Lord for the rest of her life."

She was Herma Allen Beamer. That last baby was Frank. And she kept her promise to the Lord.

Mamas often face challenges in their lives that involve their children, but no mother in history has faced a challenge to match that of Mary, whom God chose to be the mother of Jesus. Like mamas and their children throughout time, Mary experienced both joy and perplexity in her relationship with her son.

To the end, though, Mary stood by her boy. She followed him all the way to his execution, an act of love and bravery since Jesus was condemned as an enemy of the Roman Empire.

But just as mothers like Mary and Herma Beamer -- and perhaps yours -- would apparently do anything for their children, so will God do anything out of love for his children. After all, that was God on the cross at the foot of which Mary stood, and he was dying for you, one of his children.

She was just mom. She demanded you do well. She knew how to endure.
— Frank Beamer's brother, Barnett, on their mother

Mamas often sacrifice for their children,
but God, too, will do anything out of love
for his children, including dying on a cross.

MAKE NO MISTAKE

Read Mark 14:66-72.

"Then Peter remembered the word Jesus had spoken to him: 'Before the rooster crows twice you will disown me three times.' And he broke down and wept" (v. 72).

Rick Razzano and some of his Hokie teammates made a mistake one night: They figured it was a good time to have a massive water fight without getting into any trouble.

Razzano has been called "perhaps the best linebacker to ever play in Blacksburg." He was the Hokies' leading tackler all four seasons that he played (1974-77). He still holds school records for most tackles in a game (30 against Kentucky in 1977), most tackles in a season (177 in 1975 and since tied by Scott Hill in 1987), and most career tackles (634). He was inducted into the Virginia Tech Sports Hall of Fame in 1997.

Razzano lived with other athletes in Hillcrest Hall until his senior season. Naturally, pranks were an ongoing part of life in the jock dorm. Some came with a message such as the time the football players let a basketball player know he talked too much. They took off his clothes, taped him to a chair, taped his mouth shut, and rolled him out into the street. As Razzano put it, "Even the campus cops came by and were laughing."

Coach Jack White and his wife lived in the dorm to maintain some semblance of order, but one night when White was on the road recruiting, the football and basketball players threw a big

water fight, confident their hijinks would go unreported. Shortly after, though, White showed up and knocked on each door with a grim message: "I'll see you tomorrow at 7:00 in the stadium."

"He just ran and ran us to death," Razzano said. Lineman Keith Gibson, whose nickname was "Well," showed up prepared for running the stadium steps: He strapped a canteen of water to his belt buckle and periodically stopped and grabbed a swig.

It's distressing but it's true: Like Hokie athletes planning some boisterous fun and Simon Peter, we all make mistakes. Only one perfect man ever walked on this earth, and no one of us is he. Some mistakes are just dumb. Like locking yourself out of your car or falling into a swimming pool with your clothes on.

Other mistakes are more significant. Like heading down a path to addiction. Committing a crime. Walking out on a spouse and the children.

All these mistakes, however, from the momentarily annoying to the life-altering tragic, share one aspect: They can all be forgiven in Christ. Other folks may not forgive us; we may not even forgive ourselves. But God will forgive us when we call upon him in Jesus' name.

Thus, the twofold fatal mistake we can make is ignoring the fact that we will die one day and subsequently ignoring the fact that Jesus is the only way to shun Hell and enter Heaven. We absolutely must get this one right.

Coach White got the best of us that time.
-- Rick Razzano on the punishment for the water fight

Only one mistake we make sends us to Hell when we die: ignoring Jesus while we live.

DAY 65

SOMETHING NEW

Read Colossians 3:5-17.

"[S]ince you have taken off your old self with its practices and have put on the new self, which is being renewed in knowledge in the image of its Creator" (vv. 9-10).

The new kid on the block did quite well, thank you.

Most of the "experts" said that Virginia Tech would struggle when it began competition in the ACC in 2005. The conference was indeed a step up overall from Tech's previous lives as an independent, as a member of the Atlantic 10, and as a Big East school.

While expectations may have been tempered by Tech's being a conference rookie, anticipation was not; fans generally couldn't wait to get into the ACC. So just how did the new kid do that first year? So well that athletic director Jim Weaver crowed, "It's the best thing that's ever happened to this university in my opinion."

For starters, the Hokie football team turned the old league upside down by winning the championship and claiming the league's berth in the Sugar Bowl. Considering the quality of the school's signature athletic program, though, that wasn't really much of a shock. What was surprising to those not especially familiar with Hokie athletics was the breadth of Virginia Tech's accomplishments that first season.

-- The men's basketball team earned the fourth seed in the ACC Tournament.

-- The women's basketball team made the NCAA Tournament.

HOKIES

-- The women's soccer team made the NCAA Tournament.

-- The softball team made the NCAA Tournament.

-- The wrestling team finished unbeaten in ACC dual meets and was runner-up in the ACC tournament.

-- The men's soccer team beat Duke when it was ranked No. 1 and Virginia when it was ranked No. 2.

Throw in a bunch of individual awards and the new kid in town did even better than the most ardent Hokie fans expected.

New things in our lives often have a life-changing effect. A new spouse. A new baby. A new job. A new sports conference for our favorite team. Even something as mundane as a new television set or lawn mower jolts us with change.

But new experiences, new people, and new toys may make our lives new but they can't make new lives for us. Inside, where it counts – down in the deepest recesses of our soul – we're still the same, no matter how desperately we may wish to change.

An inner restlessness drives us to seek escape from a life that is a monotonous routine. Such a mundane existence just isn't good enough for someone who is a child of God; it can't even be called living. We want more out of life; something's got to change.

The only hope for a new life lies in becoming a brand new man or woman. And that is possible only through Jesus Christ, he who can make all things new again.

Overall, I'm very pleased with our inaugural campaign.
-- Tech athletic director Jim Weaver on the first year in the ACC

A brand new you with the promise of a life worth living is waiting in Jesus Christ.

HOW YOU SEE IT

Read John 20:11-18.

"Mary stood outside the tomb crying" (v. 11).

Tech's boosters were so proud of how much money they had raised that they arranged a special ceremony to present it to their new head football coach. He was so disgusted by how small the total was that he told them to keep it.

In 1951, Tech hired Bear-Bryant assistant Frank Moseley to revitalize the fortunes of the football program. (See Devotion No. 90.) Money was one of Moseley's initial concerns. In his first newsletter, he wrote, "Much money has been spent and very little or no value received." He said the team had about fifty players on scholarship, "costing about $40,000 per year, and in my way of thinking, only 21 of the 50 have any possibilities at all."

Moseley set about getting some value for that money with his "Operation Bootstrap," which ratcheted up the intensity at Tech. Center-linebacker Jack Prater, who was named to the Virginia Tech Sports Hall of Fame in 1993, said the early days of Moseley's program were "like a war, and we were the survivors."

Money was an acute problem because athletic director Henry "Puss" Redd, who coached the Hokies from 1932-40, had for some time steadfastly refused to allow the alumni to raise money for athletics as other schools were doing. With the losses mounting, however, he relented. In 1949, a group formed the Virginia Tech Student Aid Foundation to solicit contributions for athletics.

HOKIES

By the time Moseley arrived, they had raised almost $10,000, and the members were eager to meet the new coach and present the money to him. Red English, one of the founding members, recalled that at a meeting in Roanoke he "got up in front of the group and gave my little song and dance about how hard we had worked for it." Moseley's perspective was not quite the same as English's however. To everyone's shock, Moseley replied, "If that's all you got, just keep it." They raised $9,000 more on the spot.

Your perspective goes a long way toward determining whether you slink through life amid despair, anger, and hopelessness or stride boldly through life with joy and hope. Mary is a good example. On that first Easter morning, she stood by Jesus' tomb crying, her heart broken, because she still viewed everything through the perspective of Jesus' death. But how her attitude, her heart, and her life changed when she saw the morning through the perspective of Jesus' resurrection.

So it is with life and death for all of us. You can't avoid death, but you can determine how you perceive it. Is it fearful, dark, fraught with peril and uncertainty? Or is it a simple little passageway to glory, the light, and loved ones, an elevator ride to paradise?

It's a matter of perspective that depends totally on whether or not you're standing by Jesus' side when it arrives.

For some people it's the end of the rainbow, but for us it's the end of the finish line.

— Rower Larisa Healy

**Whether death is your worst enemy
or a solicitous chauffeur is a matter of perspective.**

WHO CARES?

Read Psalm 90.

"Teach us to number our days aright, that we may gain a heart of wisdom" (v. 12).

Y ou can't take anything for granted." That was the message Michael Crawford literally preached to his teammates. His life served as the example.

As a senior rover, Crawford was an inspirational leader on the field for the 8-5 Hokie team of 2003. "He's the type of leader we need on this team," said sophomore Jimmy Williams. "He's kind of like the preacher on this team."

Which is exactly what Crawford was.

The Hokies team of 2003 gathered for chapel worship services each Saturday morning before a game. Crawford handled the sermons. "I'm going to squeeze a lot of things in these guys' minds," he declared about his pulpit plans for a service. One thing was certain: When Crawford talked and delivered a message about miracles and about never taking a moment of their lives for granted, his teammates listened and they took it in.

That's because Crawford delivered his messages from more than the perspective of a teammate. As a junior, he was diagnosed with cancer of the lymph nodes. Ultimately, though, he was given a clean bill of health. Crawford has always known the source of his miraculous healing. "You talk about Jesus turning water into wine, so why can't I talk about things that he has done for me?"

he asked. "I had my life on the line. But, hey, I'm here."

Crawford knew that a number of the guys on the team took his message to heart, and that pleased him. "It shows them you can't take anything for granted," he said. Head coach Frank Beamer delivered a hearty "Amen" to that, saying, "Michael Crawford is a great lesson for a lot of us."

Our daily lives usually settle into a routine; most of us don't thrive in a state of ongoing chaos. The danger of such familiarity, however, is that we come to take for granted that which is precious in our lives. Our family members, our health, our friends, the security of our jobs. We may even become careless about them to the point of indifference.

But as Michael Crawford's experience with cancer illustrates, we can assume nothing about the permanence of anything in our lives. This includes our salvation, which all too many people take for granted. They assume that just because they know who Jesus is, because they live what the world considers to be a "good" life, and because they attend church now and then, that they are saved.

But salvation comes through a commitment to Jesus, a surrendering of our lives to his control, and a love for him that overwhelms us. Taking Jesus and our salvation for granted is a sure sign that such commitment, surrender, and love are lacking.

I always took for granted that I could play. Now I know what a gift it is.
-- Rebecca Lobo, after a knee injury

Taking Jesus for granted negates the commitment to him that is necessary for our salvation.

THE SUB

Read Galatians 3:10-14.

"Christ redeemed us from the curse of the law by becoming a curse for us" (v. 13).

Frank Beamer was already considering which end of the field he wanted to start the overtime on -- and then a sub made a play.

On Nov. 16, 1996, the 21st-ranked Hokies met Big-East foe and 18th-ranked Miami in the Orange Bowl, where Tech had never beaten the Hurricanes. This night had a real good chance of not being any different even though Tech had the lead late in the game. The Hokies took a 14-7 lead with 4:01 left in the third quarter on Michael Stuewe's diving catch of a 13-yard toss from quarterback Jim Druckenmiller and Shayne Graham's conversion.

But as the fourth quarter ran down, the Hurricanes made one last attempt to save themselves. They roared downfield, taking only 43 seconds to cover 65 yards. That set them up at the Tech 14 with 3:10 left.

"I was getting ready to say, 'Which end of the field are we going to go to in overtime,'" Beamer admitted after the game. But then the sub stepped up and changed everything.

The sub was backup free safety Keion Carpenter. He would go on to set the school record for blocked punts with five and enjoy an eight-year pro football career. On this night, though, he was a sophomore, in the lineup only because the starting safety, Torrian Gray, had moved over to cornerback in place of a true freshman.

On fourth and four from the Tech 8, the Miami quarterback "threw the ball right to me," Carpenter said about his first career interception. When Beamer saw the interception at the goal line with 1:54 left, he thought, "I wanted him to get down so we could run some time off the clock and try to end this thing." Carpenter, however, had a different idea. He took off and returned his theft 100 yards to seal the 21-7 win.

"I never thought I'd be the one to make the big play," Carpenter jubilantly said. But he did -- as a substitute.

Wouldn't it be cool if you had a substitute like Keion Carpenter for all life's hard stuff? Telling of a death in the family? Call in your sub. Breaking up with your boyfriend? Job interview? Chemistry test? Crucial presentation at work? Let the sub handle it.

We do have such a substitute, but not for the matters of life. Instead, Jesus is our substitute for matters of life and death. Since Jesus has already made it, we don't have to make the sacrifice God demands for forgiveness and salvation.

One of the ironies of our age is that many people desperately grope for a substitute for Jesus. Mysticism, human philosophies such as Scientology, false religions such as Hinduism and Islam, cults, New Age approaches that preach self-fulfillment without responsibility or accountability – they and others like them are all pitiful, inadequate substitutes for Jesus.

Who would have ever imagined Keion Carpenter?
-- Senior Tech linebacker Brandon Semones on the Miami interception

**Accept no substitutes. It's Jesus or nothing.
the consummate substitute.**

GOOD ADVICE

Read Isaiah 8:11-9:7.

"And he will be called Wonderful Counselor" (v. 9:6b).

A little brotherly advice landed Tech one of its greatest offensive linemen ever.

From 1990-93, Jim Pyne started 35 consecutive games and 41 of the 42 games in which he played. His senior season he was Tech's first unanimous All-America. In the course of his more than 2,700 snaps in Blacksburg, he allowed only one quarterback sack. His number 73 has been retired, he is in the school's hall of fame, and the offensive line meeting room is named after him. He has been described as "one of the key players in the resurgence of the Virginia Tech program" that began with the 1993 team and has never waned.

Pyne's grandfather was a two-way lineman for the Providence Steamrollers, who later became the Chicago Bears. His dad was a defensive lineman for the Boston Patriots. When Pyne played his first game in the NFL, his became the first three-generation family in NFL history.

Pyne grew up in Massachusetts, and his football exploits drew the attention of a number of colleges. A little advice from his brother to the Hokie coaches was required to land him in Blacksburg. Jim's older brother had played football at Brown University, and two of his former coaches were on Frank Beamer's staff at the time. They called Pyne's brother and asked him how they could

land his younger sibling. He advised them, "Get your head coach on an airplane and get him up here and you'll probably get him." Beamer followed his advice. Sure enough, he signed Jim Pyne.

Like the Tech coaches trying to sign Jim Pyne, we all need a little advice now and then. More often that not, we turn to professional counselors, who are all over the place. Marriage counselors, grief counselors, guidance counselors in our schools, rehabilitation counselors, all sorts of mental health and addiction counselors -- We even have pet counselors. No matter what our situation or problem, we can find plenty of advice for the taking.

The problem, of course, is that we find advice easy to offer but hard to swallow. We also have a tendency to go to the wrong source for advice, seeking counsel that doesn't really solve our problem but that instead enables us to continue with it.

Our need for outside advice, for an independent perspective on our situation, is actually God-given. God serves many functions in our lives, but one role clearly delineated in his Word is that of Counselor. Jesus himself is described as the "Wonderful Counselor." All the advice we need in our lives is right there for the asking; we don't even have to pay for it except with our faith. God is always there for us: to listen, to lead, and to guide.

I don't think you want to listen to what the fans say. If you listen to them too much, you'll be sitting up there with them.
-- Frank Beamer on taking advice from fans

We all need and seek advice in our lives, but the ultimate and most wonderful Counselor is of divine and not human origin.

OLD-FASHIONED FOLKS

Read Leviticus 18:1-5.

"You must obey my laws and be careful to follow my decrees. I am the Lord your God" (v. 4).

Showboating is unfortunately quite common among today's college athletes. That backdrop makes both what Hokie quarterback Tom Stafford did in a game to show his exasperation and his coach's subsequent rebuke seem quaint and old-fashioned.

Stafford was Tech's starting quarterback in 1966; he led the Hokies to an 8-2-1 record and a berth in the Liberty Bowl. He played defensive back his first two seasons before moving across the line because, as he put it, "there was a lag in the process of having quarterbacks come through."

The Hokies were coming off a big 23-21 win over FSU when they played Wake Forest on the road on Nov. 5. In recalling the game, Stafford said, "We didn't do much . . . but I never felt like we were in danger" of losing. Tech won 11-0.

During the game, coach Jerry Claiborne sent a play in, following the usual practice, as Stafford described it, of "tak[ing] up a lot of clock and put[ting] the pressure on the quarterbacks." This time, though, the substitute with the play showed up exceptionally late, and Stafford called a timeout to avoid a penalty. The play that came in was the same one he had already called in the huddle. In frustration, Stafford turned and kicked up some dirt before he walked back to the huddle. "I did it and didn't think

anything about it," Stafford recalled.

When the team arrived home, Claiborne told his quarterback right in front of the whole team, "I'm not too pleased with you." "What did I do?" Stafford asked. "You kicked the dirt," Claiborne replied. "You don't kick the dirt. Don't let that happen again."

It was a moment that today definitely seems old-fashioned.

Usually, when we refer to some person, some idea, or some institution as old-fashioned, we deliver a full-fledged or at least thinly veiled insult. They're out of step with the times and the mores, hopelessly out of date, totally irrelevant, and quite useless.

For the people of God, however, "old-fashioned" is exactly the lifestyle we should pursue. The throwbacks are the ones who value honor, dignity, sacrifice, and steadfastness, who can be counted on to tell the truth and to do what they say. Old-fashioned folks shape their lives according to eternal values and truths, the ones handed down by almighty God.

These ancient laws and decrees are still relevant to contemporary life because they direct us to a lifestyle of holiness and righteousness that serves us well every single day. Such a way of living allows us to escape the ultimately hopeless life to which so many have doomed themselves in the name of being modern.

I am a firm believer that if you can't get it the old-fashioned way, you don't need it.

-- Bo Jackson

**The ancient lifestyle God calls us to still leads us
to a life of contentment, peace, and joy,
which never grows old-fashioned.**

DAY 71

DRY RUN

Read John 4:1-15.

"Everyone who drinks this water will be thirsty again,
but whoever drinks the water I give him will never thirst.
Indeed, the water I give him will become in him a spring
of water welling up to eternal life" (vv. 13-14).

The drought was of biblical proportions. It lasted 93 years.

In 1917, Tech's basketball team beat N.C. State 27-18 in Raleigh. Coached by H.P. Seaborn and captained by C.L. Logan, the squad rolled to a 17-2 record that season. Only North Carolina scored 30 points or more on the Hokies; three opponents managed only single digits. Virginia Christian was trounced 59-2.

The team was less than a decade removed from the 1908-09 squad, Tech's first. Woodrow Wilson was president, and the U.S. entered World War I that year. Walt Disney graduated from high school, the Communists took power in Russia, the NHL was formed, and first-class mail was upped to 3 cents per ounce.

Tech fielded perennially strong teams in those early days. For instance, in the ten seasons from 1913-23, the Hokies went 145-44 and never had a losing season. Thus, that 1917 win over N.C. State seemed pretty routine. It was not, however, because it would be 93 years before the Hokies would whip State on the road again.

The two schools were Southern Conference rivals in the early half of the century, so they played frequently -- and every time the game was played in Raleigh, the Hokies lost. The 93-year

drought stretched across 19 straight losses.

It finally ended on Feb. 10, 2010, when the Hokies rode into town and pasted the Wolfpack 72-52 behind 23 points from Dorenzo Hudson, 15 from Malcolm Delaney, 14 from Jeff Allen, and 12 from J.T. Thompson. That the epic drought would end on this night was never in doubt; the Hokies hit their first ten shots from the field, canned their first four free throws, led 26-7 nine minutes into the game, and never looked back.

You can walk across that river you boated on in the spring. The city's put all neighborhoods on water restriction, and that beautiful lawn you fertilized and seeded will turn a sickly, pale green and may lapse all the way to brown. Somebody wrote "Wash Me" on the rear window of your truck.

The sun bakes everything, including the concrete. The earth itself seems exhausted, just barely hanging on. It's a drought.

It's the way a soul looks that shuts God out.

God instilled thirst in us to warn us of our body's need for physical water. He also gave us a spiritual thirst that can be quenched only by his presence in our lives. Without God, we are like tumbleweeds, dried out and windblown, offering the illusion of life where there is only death.

Living water – water of life – is readily available in Jesus. We may drink our fill, and thus we slake our thirst and end our soul's drought – forever.

Drink before you are thirsty. Rest before you are tired.
-- Paul de Vivie, father of French cycle touring

Our soul thirsts for God's refreshing presence.

FAITHFUL LIVES

Read Hebrews 11:1-12.

"Faith is the substance of things hoped for, the evidence of things not seen" (v. 1 NKJV).

Reality shouted that Shawn Scales didn't stand a chance in his life; the deck was stacked too high against him. Scales, though, had something on his side reality couldn't beat: He had faith.

Scales grew up on the streets with a drug-addicted mother, a drug-dealing brother, and an absent father. Both his mother and his brother served prison time for drug-related offenses. In 1988, when he was 13, Scales took a step that changed his life: He asked his middle-school coach for lunch money. Soon he was living in the coach's home. When a job change required that the coach move, Scales stayed with five different families during his high-school years. As a senior, he lived in the home of a teammate.

In football, Scales found the way out of his desperate situation. He was heavily recruited by Virginia Tech and others, but his college hopes apparently ended when he failed to achieve the minimum SAT score required for an athletic scholarship. Scales refused to give up. He scraped up enough money to pay his way at Fork Union Military Academy. When he finished there, his SAT scores were high enough; Tech offered him a scholarship.

Scales was a four-year letterman for the Hokies. He started at flanker and was a kick return specialist for the 1996 and '97 teams, his junior and senior seasons. He led the '96 team in receiving and

kickoff returns. In his career, he caught 46 passes for 821 yards, averaging 17.8 yards per reception, and scored six touchdowns, including one against Nebraska in the Orange Bowl.

"My whole life has been adversity," Scales admitted while he was at Tech. He said he refused to let the obstacles -- big as they were -- stand in his way. So what made the difference for him? He had no doubts it was his faith. "I just lean on God and pray every day to get by," Scales said. "You've got to keep the faith."

Your faith forms the heart and soul of what you are. Faith in people, things, ideologies, and concepts to a large extent determines how you spend your life, as witnessed by Shawn Scales' story. You believe in your family, in the basic goodness of the American people, in freedom and liberty, and in abiding by the law. These beliefs mold you and make you the person you are.

This is all great stuff, of course, that makes for decent human beings and productive lives. None of it, however, is as important as what you believe about Jesus. To have faith in Jesus is to believe his message of hope and salvation as recorded in the Bible. True faith in Jesus, however, has an additional component; it must also include a personal commitment to him. In other words, you don't just believe in Jesus; you live for him.

Faith in Jesus does more than shape your life; it determines your eternity.

To me, religion – faith – is the only real thing in life.
-- Bobby Bowden

Your belief system is the foundation upon which you build a life; faith in Jesus is the foundation for your eternal life.

IN THE BAD TIMES

Read Philippians 1:3-14.

*"What has happened to me has really served to advance
the gospel. . . . Because of my chains, most of the brothers
in the Lord have been encouraged to speak the word of
God more courageously and fearlessly" (vv. 12, 14).*

Today, Frank Beamer is one of the most successful and respected
coaches in college football history. Once, though, the times were
so bad at Tech that he was told to win or hit the road.

Through the 2010 season, capped by an ACC title and another
BCS bowl, Beamer's record at Virginia Tech stood at 198-95-2 and
included eighteen straight bowl appearances and seven straight
seasons of ten or more wins.

But the good times now associated with Tech football have
come after some bad times. When Beamer accepted the head
coaching job in 1987, he took over a program that was a mess.
Money was short, the Hokies would soon be on probation, and
the former head coach was suing the school. The athletic director
who hired him quit before Beamer ever coached a game.

Beamer's first team went 2-9, his second 3-8. The coach and his
team appeared to turn a corner in 1989 when they went 6-4-1, but
the next two seasons were mediocre at 6-5 and 5-6. Still, that was
better than the 1992 disaster with its dismal 2-8-1 record. After six
seasons, Beamer's record was an unacceptable 24-40-2; his future
at Tech was anything but secure.

In 1993, a 9-3 record that included a win over Indiana in the Independence Bowl seemed a harbinger of better times. By now, though, the administration at Tech wasn't sure. AD Dave Braine delivered an ultimatum to Beamer: Win six games in 1994 and we'll renew your contract; have a losing season and we won't.

The Hokies went 8-4 and have never looked back. Today, Tech football, good times, and Frank Beamer are synonymous.

Loved ones die. You're downsized. Your biopsy looks cancerous. Your spouse could be having an affair. Hard, tragic times are as much a part of life as breath.

This applies to Christians too. Christianity is not the equivalent of a Get-out-of-Jail-Free card, granting us a lifelong exemption from either the least or the worst pain the world has to offer. While Jesus promises us he will be there to lead us through the valleys, he never promises that we will not enter them.

The question thus becomes how you handle the bad times. You can buckle to your knees in despair and cry, "Why me?" Or you can hit your knees in prayer and ask, "What do I do with this?"

Setbacks and tragedies are opportunities to reveal and to develop true character and abiding faith. Your faithfulness -- not your skipping merrily along through life without pain -- is what reveals the depth of your love for God.

There were days when I'm sure a lot of people wondered if [success at Virginia Tech] was possible.

— Frank Beamer

**Faithfulness to God requires faith even in --
especially in -- the bad times.**

JUMPING FOR JOY

Read Luke 6:20-26.

"Rejoice in that day and leap for joy, because great is your reward in heaven" (v. 23).

I t's a jumping thing." So did head coach Frank Beamer describe a key play by Jeff King that turned a close game into a rout.

On Sept. 24, 2005, King, a senior tight end, quite literally had a hand in Virginia Tech's first two scores against Georgia Tech. When he hauled in a 13-yard touchdown pass from Marcus Vick in the first quarter, King set a school record. It was the ninth touchdown of his career, the most ever by a tight end. He had held the record with Ken Barefoot (1965-67) and Steve Johnson (1984-87).

That catch jumped the Hokies out to a 7-0 lead. His next big play came later in the first quarter on a try for a 35-yard field goal by the Yellow Jackets. King, who is 6-foot-5, teamed with Duane Brown, also 6-5, to anchor the middle of the Hokie defensive line on field goals. "Anytime you've got two tall guys in there like me and Duane, we have a lot better shot at blocking it than [tailback Mike] Imoh," King pointed out. Imoh stood 5-7.

That approach certainly paid dividends this time. The Tech offensive guard stepped inside to block Brown, leaving King free to hop over the guard's leg and block the kick. D.J. Parker scooped up the loose ball and sprinted 78 yards for a touchdown that took most of the fight out of the Jackets. They were never in the game

after that as the Hokies won going away 51-7.

The block was King's third at Tech, and his basketball background, both in high school and on the Hokie squad, certainly was a factor in his success. At least Beamer thought so. "Probably his basketball skills there help him a little bit because it's a jumping thing," Beamer said.

You're probably a pretty good jumper yourself when the Hokies score. You just can't help it. It's like your feet and your seat have suddenly become magnets that repel each other. The sad part is that you always come back down to earth; the moment of exultation passes.

But what if you could jump for joy all the time? Not literally, of course; you'd pass out from exhaustion. But figuratively, with your heart aglow and joyous even when life is its most difficult.

Joy is an absolutely essential component of the Christian life. Not only do we experience joy in our public praise and worship – which is temporary – but we live daily in the joy that comes from the presence of God in our lives and the surety of his saving power extended to us through Jesus Christ.

It's not happiness, which derives from external factors; it's joy, which comes from inside.

No one can say 'You must not run faster than this, or jump higher than that.' The human spirit is indomitable.
-- Sir Roger Bannister, first to run a sub-4-minute mile

Unbridled joy can send you jumping all over the place; life in Jesus means such exultation is not rare but rather is a way of life.

DAY 75

WHOLEHEARTEDLY

Read 1 Samuel 13:1-14.

"The Lord has sought out a man after his own heart" (v. 14).

The greatest team in Tech women's basketball history obviously was loaded with talent. But on a night when they seemed to be doomed to a surprise defeat, they showed they had plenty of heart to go with that talent.

The Hokies of 1998-99 went 28-3, a school record for wins that still stands. They won the Atlantic 10 championship, losing only once during the regular season. In the quarterfinals of the league tournament, though, they were in a heap of trouble.

It all started the night before the game when coach Bonnie Henrickson decided senior point guard and team leader Lisa Weatherspoon wasn't able to play. Because of painful back spasms, she couldn't even bend over to tie her shoes. Henrickson admitted, "The decision that was best for Lisa Weatherspoon is certainly not what's best for our basketball team."

She was dead right. "Without the scrappy Witherspoon, their unquestioned heart and soul," the Hokies didn't show up. Dayton, a team they had already beaten twice, rolled to a 37-21 lead with 15:39 left to play. The team "was totally out of sync."

Maybe so, but it still had heart. "At that point we had nothing to lose," said senior forward Michelle Houseright. "So we said, 'OK, we've got to take control.'" And they did. The Hokies turned

up the defensive pressure and the offensive intensity, caught the Flyers at 47 with 1:35 left to play, and sent the game into OT.

And a second OT. And a third OT. The Hokies appeared to have the game won in the second overtime, but their heart was tested again when Dayton nailed a trey with five seconds left to tie it. In the third extra period, senior forward Katie O'Connor hit a free throw with 5.8 seconds that made the difference. With all the heart they could muster, the Hokies had come from 16 points down, played on into three overtimes, and claimed a 73-72 win.

We all face defeat. Sometimes, even though we fight with all we have, we lose. Even Tech loses games.

At some time, you probably have admitted you were whipped no matter how much it hurt. Always in your life, though, you have known that you would fight for some things with all your heart and never give them up: your family, your country, your friends, your core beliefs.

God should be on that list too. God seeks men and women who will never turn their back on him because they are people after God's own heart. That is, they will never betray God with their unbelief; they will never lose their childlike trust in God; they will never cease to love God with all their heart.

They are lifetime members of God's team; it's a mighty good one to be on, but it takes heart.

This team won't quit; it never has at anything.
-- Head coach Bonnie Henrickson on her 1998-99 squad

To be on God's team
requires the heart of a champion.

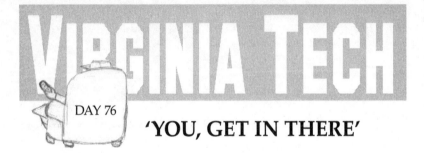

DAY 76

'YOU, GET IN THERE'

Read 1 Samuel 3:1-18.

"The Lord came and stood there, calling as at the other times, 'Samuel! Samuel!' Then Samuel said, 'Speak, for your servant is listening'" (v. 10).

Y ou, get in there!" With that less than poetic calling from a Virginia Tech coach who didn't even know his name, Tom Beasley's football career began in earnest.

Beasley showed up in Blacksburg in the fall of 1973 with aspirations of being an offensive lineman. The truth was, however, that he was pretty awful. "I was like, fifth-, sixth-, or seventh-team," he recalled. "I just didn't have a lot going on playing on the offensive side of the ball." The coaches tried, bouncing him around from guard, to center, to tackle. Nothing worked.

At one preseason scrimmage, though, a number of defensive tackles were injured. When head coach Charlie Coffey yelled at defensive tackles coach Carl Ellis to get somebody out there because he was holding up the scrimmage, Ellis replied, "Charlie, that's it. We don't have any more defensive tackles." Still, though, Ellis had to have a body.

At the time, Beasley happened to be standing next to Ellis. "He looked at me, trying to remember my name, but he didn't know it," Beasley said. "You could just see the wheels grinding in his head." Finally, in desperation, Ellis grabbed Beasley's jersey and bellowed, "You, get in there!"

HOKIES

The scrimmage had only about ten plays left, and Beasley got to the ball on practically every play. As he left the field, he saw Coffey and Ellis talking. Ellis then came over to Beasley and said, "Tom, you're going to be working with the varsity defensive tackles starting tomorrow."

Two games into the season, Beasley was a starter. He started four seasons (1973-76), was drated in 1977 in the third round by the Pittsburgh Steelers, and played on two Super Bowl championship teams. And it all began because he answered the call.

Something quite similar to what Tom Beasley experienced at Tech occurs when God places a specific call upon a Christian's life. When God calls, however, the ramifications are inevitably much scarier than shifting positions on a football team.

The way many folks understand it is that answering God's call means going into the ministry, packing the family up, and moving halfway around the world to some place where folks have never heard of air conditioning, paved roads, donuts, or the Hokies. Zambia. The Philippines. Cleveland even.

Not for you, no thank you. And who can blame you?

But God usually calls folks to serve him where they are. In fact, God put you where you are right now, and he has a purpose in placing you there. Like Samuel, wherever you are, no matter what age you are, you are called to serve him.

It was like being in a foreign country.
-- Welsh soccer player Ian Rush on playing in Italy

**God calls you to serve him right now
right where he has put you, wherever that is.**

DAY 77

CLOTHES HORSE

Read Genesis 37:1-11.

"Israel loved Joseph more than all his children, because he was the son of his old age: and he made him a coat of many colours" (v. 3 KJV).

A suit of clothes forever changed the history of Tech athletics.

John Moody serves Tech from his obscurely named position of senior assistant to the director of the Virginia Tech Athletic Fund. He raises money for athletics, and over almost four decades he has proved to be very good at it. He is so good that in 2008 the National Association of Athletic Development Directors awarded him its highest honor, the Lifetime Achievement Award.

Moody came to VT in 1972 as a field representative. He started out the hard way, going door-to-door asking folks for donations to the Student Aid Association. "John Moody is singularly responsible for a lot of the things that are here at the university," once said alumnus Jay Poole, who participates in Moody's annual fund-raising golf outings.

But Moody wasn't responsible for a part of the campus that bears his name. The round of renovations to Lane Stadium/Worsham Field completed in 2006 required that a flagpole outside the stadium be moved. In its place is an eye-catching flagpole and plaza that was named Moody Plaza in Moody's honor.

Moody originally had no plans to attend Tech. In 1952, he was all set to play college football for Washington & Lee until he

learned that all male students had to wear coats and ties on campus. Moody owned one sport coat and two ties, so he figured he'd better look elsewhere. Tech caught his attention because the all-military school would furnish him a cadet uniform; it wasn't a suit but it would do. Moody lettered four years.

Tech fans ever since have been grateful that a young John Moody had such a limited clothes budget.

Contemporary society proclaims that it's all about the clothes. Buy that new suit or dress, those new shoes, and all the sparkling accessories, and you'll be a new person. The changes are only cosmetic, though; under those clothes, you're the same person. Consider Joseph, for instance, prancing about in his pretty new clothes; he was still a spoiled little tattletale whom his brothers detested enough to sell into slavery.

Jesus never taught that we should run around half-naked or wear only second-hand clothes from the local mission. He did warn us, though, against making consumer items such as clothes a priority in our lives. A follower of Christ seeks to emulate Jesus not through material, superficial means such as wearing special clothing like a robe and sandals. Rather, the disciple desires to match Jesus' inner beauty and serenity -- whether the clothes the Christian wears are the sables of a king or the rags of a pauper.

It's amazing how the smallest things can dictate a decision that impacts you for the rest of your life.
-- John Moody on his decision to come to Tech because of clothes

**Where Jesus is concerned,
clothes don't make the person; faith does.**

DAY 78

TOP SECRET

Read Romans 2:1-16.

"This will take place on the day when God will judge men's secrets through Jesus Christ, as my gospel declares" *(v. 16).*

The starting right halfback for the 1900 Tech football team was Walter Brown. The player had a secret, though; Walter Brown didn't exist.

Hunter Carpenter was the greatest of Virginia Tech's early football players, the one most responsible for the landmark 11-0 win over Virginia in 1905, Tech's first-ever win in the series. He entered Tech in the fall of 1898 when he was only 15 years old, having never played football. He was immediately fascinated by it and answered Coach C.P. "Sally" Miles' call for players. Carpenter weighed only 128 pounds, though, and, not surprisingly, Miles told him he was too small for the team.

The setback did nothing to cool Carpenter's ardor for the game. He "put cleats on a pair of old shoes, donned a sweater and a pair of old football pants, and waited patiently behind the scrub team as it scrimmaged the varsity." His second season he weighed in at 150 pounds and made the team but didn't play much.

Then in 1900, he was the starting right halfback. For all three seasons, though, Carpenter had played under the pseudonym Walter Brown. He had a very good reason for keeping his real name a secret: His father had forbidden him to play football.

Not until the 50-5 smashing of the VMI Keydets in Norfolk was his identity discovered. Brought to the game by a friend, Carpenter's father watched incredulously as his son was the star. Young Carpenter was "aglow with victory" after the game when he unexpectedly ran into his dad in a hotel lobby. His father was so impressed by his son's performance, though, that he relented, advising his son to do his best when he played.

We all have secrets or at least personal information we don't want being made public. Much information about us -- from credit reports to what movies we rent -- is readily available to prying and persistent persons. In our information age, people we don't know may know a lot about us — or at least they can find out. And some of them may use this information for harm.

While diligence may allow us to be reasonably successful in keeping some secrets from the world at large, we should never deceive ourselves into believing we are keeping secrets from God. God knows everything about us, including the things we wouldn't want proclaimed at church. All our sins, mistakes, failures, short-comings, quirks, prejudices, and desires – God knows all our would-be secrets.

But here's something God hasn't kept a secret: No matter what he knows about us, he loves us still.

The secret to winning football games is working more as a team and less as individuals.
— Knute Rockne

We have no secrets before God, and it's no secret
that he nevertheless loves us still.

DAY 79

HOME-FIELD ADVANTAGE

Read Joshua 24:14-27.

"Choose for yourselves this day whom you will serve. . . .
But as for me and my household, we will serve the Lord"
(v. 15).

From the naked professor to a ceiling that scared the daylights out of opposing divers, War Memorial Gymnasium was a vital part of the development of Virginia Tech athletics -- but most of all it was quite a home-field advantage.

The old facility hosted its last intercollegiate event on Jan. 16, 2010. Fittingly, the swimming and diving team defeated Davidson College, thus bringing to a close 85 years of Virginia Tech sports history. The building originally served as the home for the basketball team; it also housed the football locker rooms until the late 1960s. The swimming pool was not even part of the original design, but was added in 1932.

The naked professor is one of the building's legends. History says that he came in after the swim team practiced and swam before the pool reopened for all the students. Recalled one alumnus, "If a coed came in early and saw [the naked professor] swimming, he would get out of the pool stark naked . . . and say, 'The pool doesn't reopen until 7 p.m. if you want to come back then.'"

Bill Beecher, who swam for Tech in the 1970s and started the Virginia Tech women's swimming program in 1976, recalled his first encounter with the naked professor: "There he was swimming

on the other end of the pool naked. It was quite a shock."

The building's pool provided a home-field advantage in a rather unique way. "We only had a one-meter board for diving," Beecher recalled, "and when the divers dove they went up between the rafters. It scared a lot of teams that came in there."

The old gymnasium was such an advantage that Tech was able, as veteran Hokie swimming and diving coach Ned Skinner put it, to build a top-25 program "out of a closet."

You enter your home to find love, security, and joy. It's the place where your heart feels warmest, your laughter comes easiest, and your life is its richest. It is the center of and the reason for everything you do and everything you are.

How can a home be such a place?

If it is a home where grace is spoken before every meal, it is such a place. If it is a home where the Bible is read, studied, and discussed by the whole family gathered together, it is such a place. If it is a home that serves as a jumping-off point for the whole family to go to church, not just on Sunday morning and not just occasionally, but regularly, it is such a place. If it is a home where the name of God is spoken with reverence and awe and not with disrespect and indifference, it is such a place.

In other words, a house becomes a true home when God is part of the family.

It was definitely a great home-field advantage.
-- 2010 Tech swim captain Chip Hughes on War Memorial Gymnasium

A home is full when all the family members –
including God -- are present.

UNEXPECTEDLY

Read Matthew 24:36-51.

"No one knows about that day or hour, not even the angels in heaven, nor the Son, but only the Father" (v. 36).

Right smack dab in the middle of a serious de-emphasis on athletics in general and football in particular, Virginia Tech did something totally unexpected: The Hokies produced one of their greatest teams ever.

In the late 1920s and early 1930s, a general lack of interest in athletics permeated Virginia Tech. Not a single football scholarship was awarded in 1932 as the athletic program was in decline and athletic officials didn't seem to care. "We just weren't keeping up with the times," recalled Herbert "Mac" MacEver, part of Tech's legendary "Pony Express" backfield from 1925-28. "Everybody else had organizations going. They were getting money from alumni and going commercial. They were getting scholarships and going out and finding players."

But not Virginia Tech. Athletic Director C.P. "Sally" Miles said in a speech that the object of athletes was not necessarily to win "but to fight in a gentlemanly way." Henry "Puss" Redd, Tech's head football coach, agreed, declaring how discouraging it was to see a young man excel on the athletic field but fail to graduate. Rather than deal with that attitude, a group of Southern schools broke away from the Southern Conference, of which Miles was the president, and formed the Southeastern Conference.

HOKIES

As the debate raged about the proper role of athletics at Tech, the 1932 football team unexpectedly produced one of the school's great seasons. Since he had no scholarships to hand out, Redd held open tryouts among the corps of cadets and managed to find 24 players for a traveling squad. With a team made up of what Mac-Ever called "smart kids, not really athletes," the Hokies went 8-1 and whipped Georgia, Kentucky, Maryland, and Virginia. The only loss was 9-6 to Alabama in Tuscaloosa.

We think we've got everything figured out and under control, and then something unexpected happens. About the only thing we can expect from life with any certainty is the unexpected.

God is that way too, suddenly showing up to remind us he's still around. A friend who calls and tells you he's praying for you, a hug from your child or grandchild, a lone lily that blooms in your yard -- unexpected moments when the divine comes crashing into our lives with such clarity that it takes our breath away and brings tears to our eyes.

But why shouldn't God do the unexpected? The only factor limiting what God can do in our lives is the paucity of our own faith. We should expect the unexpected from God, this same deity who caught everyone by surprise by unexpectedly coming to live among us as a man, and who will return when we least expect it.

When I look back on it, I don't know how we did it.
— E.R. "Red" English, a guard on the 8-1 1932 team

God continually does the unexpected,
like showing up as Jesus,
who will return unexpectedly.

DAY 81

I CAN'T STAND IT!

Read Exodus 32:1-20.

"[Moses'] anger burned and he threw the tablets out of his hands, breaking them to pieces at the foot of the mountain" (v. 19).

How in the world could a game in which you score 77 points, the most in Lane Stadium history, and win by fifty points be frustrating? Well, it all depends which side of the ball you play on.

On Oct. 14, 1995, the Hokies buried the Akron Zips 77-27. As writer Randy King put it, "Akron (1-5) had one chance against Tech (4-2). It was called Zip." The Hokies led 26-0 after the first period. "I was done after one quarter," said starting quarterback Jim Druckenmiller. "We were calculating it then and we should have hit 120 points." The score ran to 47-0 at halftime on the way to the total of 77, which wiped out the previous stadium high of 59, set in a 59-21 slaughter of William and Mary in 1983.

The Hokies finished with 638 yards of total offense, third best in school history. And it wasn't like coach Frank Beamer was running up the score. He started benching his regulars early in the second quarter and "played virtually everybody on the Hokies' sideline but the water boys."

So how could such an afternoon at the office be frustrating? It has to do with the 27 points the Zips put up on four consecutive possessions in the third and fourth quarters against the Hokies second- and third-string defense. The defense came into the game

fourth in the nation in fewest points allowed; to watch the points add up was downright frustrating for the starters. "After you see all those points go up, all of us wanted to go back in," said end Lawrence Lewis. "When we saw them scoring, [the starters] said like, 'Hey, stop taking advantage of young guys.'"

While the Tech defensive starters may have been a little frustrated, their discomfort was nothing like what the Zips endured.

The traffic light catches you when you're running late for work or your doctor's appointment. The bureaucrat gives you red tape when you want assistance. Your daughter refuses to take her homework seriously. Makes your blood boil, doesn't it?

Frustration is part of God's testing ground that is life even if much of what frustrates us today results from man-made organizations, bureaucracies, and machines. What's important is not that you encounter frustration—that's a given—but how you handle it. Do you respond with curses, screams, and violence? Or with a deep breath, a silent prayer, and calm persistence, and patience?

It may be difficult to imagine Jesus stuck in traffic or waiting for hours in a long line in a government office. It is not difficult, however, to imagine how he would act in such situations, and, thus, to know exactly how you should respond. No matter how frustrated you are.

It's real frustrating. But I'm glad to see the younger guys get in there and play, because we're going to need them.
-- End Lawrence Lewis on watching Akron score 27 points

Frustration is a vexing part of life,
but God expects us to handle it gracefully.

THOSE THINGS

Read Isaiah 55:6-13.

"For my thoughts are not your thoughts, neither are your ways my ways" (v. 8).

Every team gets a few bad breaks during a season. But how about a whole year that amounts to one big bad break? Such was the fate of the 2000 Hokie baseball team.

"I've never seen a year like this. Not even close." So spoke Virginia Tech head baseball coach Chuck Hartman -- and he was in his 41st season of coaching college baseball. The "year like this" was punctuated by player suspensions and freak injuries and even the death of a player's mother.

The team finished the regular season 31-23-2. They headed into the Atlantic 10 tournament without four of their top five starting pitchers. Hartman knew sophomore Jason Bush would start the first game, but didn't know who would pitch the second contest.

One of the four missing pitchers was lost to academic problems before the season even started. Another was suspended for the season after a run-in with Hartman. All-American pitcher-first baseman Larry Bowles, the club's best hitter at .390 in 1999, went down for the year with a knee injury two games into the season. He hurt the knee slipping on ice while fishing. Freshman Joe Saunders stepped up to go 9-2, and then he was sidelined with mononucleosis.

In addition, starters Chris Hutchison (outfielder) and Christian

Simmers (second base) missed most of the second half of the seasons with injuries.

So, after a season of those things, Hartman approached the league tournament with the perspective that "We're going to roll 'em out there and see what happens." What happened was that the Hokies won it and claimed a berth in the NCAA tournament.

You've probably had a few of "those things" in your own life: bad breaks that occur without regard to justice, morality, or fair play. You wonder if everything in life is random with events determined by a chance roll of some cosmic dice. Is there really somebody scripting all this with logic and purpose?

Yes, there is; God is the author of everything.

We know how it all began; we even know how it all will end. It's in God's book. The part we play in God's kingdom, though, is in the middle, and that part is still being revealed. The simple truth is that God's ways are different from ours. After all he's God and we are not. That's why we don't know what's coming our way, and why "those things" catch us by surprise and dismay us when they do occur.

What God asks of us is that we trust him. As the one – and the only one – in charge, he knows everything will be all right for those who follow Jesus.

Despite all we've gone through, we're still not done yet.
-- Coach Chuck Hartman prior to the 2000 A-10 tournament

Life confounds us because, while we know the
end and the beginning of God's great story, we are
part of the middle, which God is still revealing.

DAY 83

NO GETTING OVER IT

Read Ephesians 2:1-10.

"It is by grace you have been saved, through faith -- and this not from yourselves, it is the gift of God -- not by works, so that no one can boast" (vv. 8-9).

I guess I've replayed that Dayton game over in my mind a hundred times."

So spoke Glen Combs, a starting guard on the 1967 Hokie basketball team that became the first team in history from the state of Virginia to make the final eight of the NCAA Tournament. But what Combs and some of his teammates really never got over was that they didn't beat Dayton and make it to the Final Four.

The 1967 team put Virginia Tech basketball on the map. The 1965-66 squad had gone 19-5 and had lost in the first round of the NIT, the first postseason basketball appearance in Tech history. But Combs and forwards Ron Perry and Ted Ware returned to lead a team that could run and could shoot.

The Hokies were one of nine independents that made the 23-team NCAA Tournament field. They met Toledo in the opening round and avenged a regular-season loss with an 82-76 win behind 24 points and 19 rebounds from sophomore center Ken Talley. Tech then beat Indiana 79-70, and suddenly, the Hokies were one win away from the Final Four. It didn't happen.

Against Dayton, the Hokies pretty much had the game under control with a ten-point lead and only 8:11 left to play. But the

HOKIES

Flyers scored nine straight points and eventually sent the game into overtime and won it 71-66. "We just kind of self-destructed going down the wire," Combs said.

So, despite the most successful season in Tech basketball history to that point, the Hokies really never got over the loss that kept them from the Final Four. It was "pretty devastating," Perry said, more than forty years after the fact. Decades later, Charlie Moir, then an assistant coach, said ruefully, "We should've won."

Like a loss in a big game, some things in life have a way of getting under your skin and never letting go. Your passion may have begun the first time you rode in a convertible. Or when your breath was taken away the first time you saw the one who would become your spouse. You knew you were hooked the first time you walked into Lane Stadium on game day.

You can put God's love on that list too. Once you encounter it in the person of Jesus Christ, you never get over it. That's because when you sincerely give your life to Jesus by acknowledging him as the Lord of your life, God's love – his grace – changes you. It sets you free to live in peace and in joy, free from the fear of death's apparent victory.

When you meet Jesus, you're never the same again. You just never get over the experience.

You spend a good deal of your life gripping a baseball, and it turns out it was the other way around all the time.
-- Former pitcher Jim Bouton

Some things hit you so hard you're never the same again; meeting Jesus is like that.

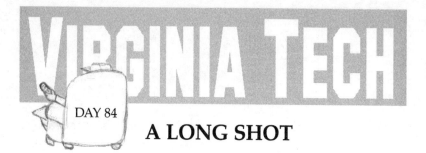

A LONG SHOT

Read Matthew 9:9-13.

"[Jesus] saw a man named Matthew sitting at the tax collector's booth. 'Follow me,' he told him, and Matthew got up and followed him" (v. 9).

Cody Grimm was such a long shot to play major college football that even he knew it. After all, big-time programs don't issue many calls for 175-pound strong safeties.

Despite Grimm's successful resume as a high-school player, William and Mary was the only college to offer him a scholarship. He would have snapped up an offer from James Madison. "Big school, bunch of girls, and I heard it was a good time," he said. But W&M was just too small, even for a long shot.

So Grimm accepted a walk-on offer from Virginia Tech, where his older brother, Chad, was on the team. Even then, long shot that he was, Grimm harbored few visions of gridiron glory. "I was just happy to be dressing and on the roster, hanging around the guys," he said. "I thought I would always play just special teams and . . . be a backup my whole career pretty much."

It started out that way. After redshirting in 2005, Grimm spent most of the next two seasons on various special teams units. But everything gradually began to change. Grimm was always a hard worker, but he worked not just on the field and at practice, but in the weight room. Gradually, he began to bulk up.

When starter Cam Martin was slowed by a bad knee, Grimm

wound up in the lineup at outside linebacker for most of the 2008 season. The long shot blossomed into a star. Grimm was the team's third-leading tackler. His senior season -- 2009 -- he started every game, was three times the ACC Player of the Week, and was first-team All-ACC and third-team All-America.

Cody Grimm the long shot had indeed come a long way.

Matthew the tax collector was another long shot, an unlikely person to be a confidant of the Son of God. While we may not get all warm and fuzzy about the IRS, our government's revenue agents are nothing like Matthew and his ilk. He bought a franchise, paying the Roman Empire for the privilege of extorting, bullying, and stealing everything he could from his own people. Tax collectors of the time were "despicable, vile, unprincipled scoundrels."

And yet, Jesus said only two words to this lowlife: "Follow me." Jesus knew that this long shot would make an excellent disciple.

It's the same with us. While we may not be quite as vile as Matthew was, none of us can stand before God with our hands clean and our hearts pure. We are all impossibly long shots to enter God's Heaven. That is, until we do what Matthew did: get up and follow Jesus.

It feels good to have the kind of success I have had. I never really expected this. It's really cool.

-- Cody Grimm

**Only through Jesus does our status change
from being long shots to enter God's Kingdom
to being heavy favorites.**

THE GREATEST

Read Mark 9:33-37.

"If anyone wants to be first, he must be the very last, and the servant of all" (v. 35).

More than three decades later, it may still be the greatest goal-line stand in Virginia Tech football history.

On Oct. 4, 1975, the Hokies limped into Auburn to take on the favored Tigers. Tech was off to a 1-2 start that included a loss to Kent State. With games against FSU and Virginia still ahead, the season was pretty much on the line down in Alabama.

Tech played its best game of the season. Both Roscoe Coles, who remains Tech's third all-time career rushing leader with 3,459 yards, and Phil Rogers, Tech's ninth all-time career rushing leader, rushed for more than 100 yards against the Auburn defense. The Hokies took a 23-16 lead late into the fourth quarter.

But Auburn made one last charge. With 4:06 left, the Tigers took over on their own 20. They steadily advanced up the field; with only 1:25 on the clock, they perched on the Tech 5-yard line. What followed was described by middle linebacker Rick Razzano as "maybe the greatest stand in Virginia Tech history. I guarantee you it was the stand of the century."

On first down, Auburn tried the middle, running right at Razzano, Tech's all-time leading tackler with 634. He stuffed the Tiger runner for no gain; lineman Bill Houseright did the same thing on second down.

Making no headway against the middle of the Tech defense, Auburn tried a third-down pass that fell incomplete. The Tigers tried a pass again on fourth down, but Razzano and Houseright and some of their closest friends chased the Auburn quarterback out of the pocket and out of bounds at the four.

Tech took over with 28 seconds to play and took a knee for the win -- after the defense's greatest goal-line stand ever.

We all want to be the greatest. The goal for the Hokies and their fans every season is the national championship. The competition at work is to be the most productive sales person on the staff or the Teacher of the Year. In other words, we define being the greatest in terms of the struggle for personal success. It's nothing new; Jesus' disciples saw greatness in the same way.

As Jesus illustrated, though, greatness in the Kingdom of God has nothing to do with the world's understanding of success. Rather, the greatest are those who channel their ambition toward the furtherance of Christ's kingdom through love and service, rather than their own advancement, which is a complete reversal of status and values as the world sees them.

After all, who could be greater than the person who has Jesus for a brother and God for a father? And that's every one of us.

That was the greatest display of guts and sportsmanship I've ever been associated with.
-- Tech head coach Jimmy Sharpe on the goal-line stand against Auburn

**To be great for God has nothing to do with
personal advancement and everything to do with
the advancement of Christ's kingdom.**

LOVE OF YOUR LIFE

Read 1 John 4:7-21.

"Whoever does not love does not know God, because God is love" (v. 8).

Virginia Tech landed one of its greatest athletes of the 1950s, an eventual Hall of Fame member, because he was in love.

Leo Burke is one of the most versatile athletes in Hokie history. He was a standout running back and fullback from 1952-55, a star on the great undefeated team of 1954. He played basketball his freshman and sophomore years and was a star outfielder for the Hokie baseball team for four seasons, leading the squad to the NCAA Tournament in 1954. He gave up basketball only because the time that playing three sports required left him struggling to keep up academically.

After graduation from Tech, Burke went on to a professional baseball career that lasted nine seasons, three in the majors where he played every position except pitcher.

Virginia Tech had the early lead in its recruitment of Burke because his high school football coach, Mel Henry, had played and coached at Tech. When Burke was a sophomore in high school, Henry took him along on a recruiting trip to Blacksburg. Burke said he "fell in love with the campus."

But love of another sort was what really clinched the deal for him. While he was still in high school, he met a young lady named Judy from a nearby town, and they fell head over heels in

love. They made plans to marry after she graduated from high school. As Burke considered his options, several of the schools recruiting him the heaviest had rules prohibiting their student-athletes from marrying. Tech had no such rule.

Love won out. Tech landed one of its greatest athletes and Burke landed the love of his life, his wife for more than fifty years.

Your heart rate accelerates, your blood pressure jumps, your mouth runs dry, your vision blurs, and you start stammering. Either you've got the flu or the one you're in love with just walked into the room and smiled at you. Fortunately, if the attraction is based on more than hormones and eye candy, the feverish frenzy that characterizes newfound love matures into a deeper, more meaningful affection. If it didn't, we'd probably die from exhaustion, stroke, heart failure, or a combination thereof.

We pursue true love with a desperation and a ferocity that is unmatched by any other desire. Ultimately, the Christian life is about that same search, about falling in love and becoming a partner in a deep-seated, satisfying, ever-growing and ever-deepening relationship. The Christian life is about loving so fiercely and so completely that love is not something we're in but something we are. The object of our love is the greatest and most faithful lover of them all: God.

I can't adequately describe to you the love that permeates a good football team.

— Joe Paterno

**God is head-over-heels in love with you;
like any lover, he wants you to return the love.**

GIFT-WRAPPED

Read James 1:12-18.

"Every good and perfect gift is from above, coming down from the Father of the heavenly lights" (v. 17).

Amy Wetzel's parents did something extraordinary for her, so she reciprocated with a very special gift: She had the game of her young career.

Wetzel is one of the greatest players in the history of Virginia Tech women's basketball. From 1996-2001 (She was redshirted her first year because of an injury.), Wetzel scored 1,444 points, sixth all-time, became Tech's all-time leader in both games and minutes played, set a school record with 489 free throws made, and finished second in school history with 235 steals and third all-time with 399 career assists. In 2000, she was the Atlantic-10 Defensive Player of the Year. She led the 1998-99 team to a 28-3 record, the highest win total in school history, and into the Sweet 16. In 2008, she was honored as an ACC Legend.

Most of Wetzel's accomplishments were ahead of her, though, on March 14, 1998, when the underdog Hokie women took on the big, bad Wisconsin Badgers in the opening round of the NCAA Tournament. The 21-9 Hokies were hot, riding a seven-game win streak. Still, they weren't expected to do much against the bigger, more physical team from the Big 10.

But Wetzel had some extra incentive to play well. Her parents drove seventeen hours from Ashland, Penn., to Gainesville, Fla.,

for the game. Inspired by their presence, she gave them a gift in return. She scored a career-high 28 points and grabbed a team-high eight rebounds to lead Tech past the shell-shocked Badgers 75-64.

"I went out there and I was just fired up," the freshman guard said after playing the game of her young life. "It was a kind of feeling I've never really felt in me." The result was not just a gift for her parents, but for her teammates and Hokie fans as well.

Receiving a gift is nice, but giving has its pleasures too, doesn't it? The children's excitement on Christmas morning. That smile of pure delight on your spouse's face when you came up with a really cool anniversary present. Your dad's surprise that time you didn't give him a tie or socks. There really does seem to be something to this being more blessed to give than to receive.

No matter how generous we may be, though, we are grumbling misers compared to God, who is the greatest gift-giver of all. That's because all the good things in our lives – every one of them – come from God. Friends, love, health, family, the air we breathe, the sun that warms us, even our very lives are all gifts from a profligate God. And here's the kicker: He even gives us eternal life with him through the gift of his son.

What in the world can we possibly give God in return? Our love and our life.

I knew I had to do something good for [my parents].
— Amy Wetzel after leading Tech over Wisconsin

Nobody can match God for giving, but you can give him the gift of your love in appreciation.

DAY 88

WEATHERPROOFED

Read Nahum 1:3-9.

"His way is in the whirlwind and the storm, and clouds are the dust of his feet" (v. 3b).

It was the first, the last, and the only time that Mark Cox has worn pantyhose.

They weren't pantyhose at all; they were tights, insisted Marie Dooley, wife of Bill Dooley. The former Tech head coach fondly disagreed. "You and I know them as pantyhose," he said. "I was wearing a pair of those suckers myself. Had 'em on under my pants. Nobody ever knew."

Pantyhose or tights, the Hokies' rather cross-dressing attire was Dooley's idea, but he obviously had a very good reason for it: It was cold, bitterly cold, when the Hokies met Virginia on Thanksgiving night in 1982. Temperature at game time was 39 degrees and was below freezing when the game ended sometime around 11:30 p.m. The game was moved to an evening kickoff for presentation on a newfangled cable station called WTBS.

Cox, the Tech quarterback, was not at all happy with his warm weather gear. "They were too hot," he said. "We were sweating so much, we had to pull them off."

Dooley not only used pantyhose to help his players withstand the cold, but he had temporary dugouts installed behind the benches.

The weather probably was a big factor in holding down the

size of the crowd, officially listed as 23,800. Even the students didn't brave the cold, picking up little more than one-fourth of their allotted tickets.

Despite the weather, the Hokies won 21-14. UVa led 7-6 at halftime, Tech's score coming on a pass from Cox to Mike Shaw. Tech led 15-14 in the third quarter when a Cox run put the final tally on the scoreboard -- as the temperature continued to drop.

A thunderstorm washes away your golf game or the picnic with the kids. Lightning knocks out the electricity just as you settle in at the computer. A tornado interrupts your Sunday dinner and sends everyone scurrying to the hallway. A hurricane cancels your beach trip.

For all our technology and our knowledge, we are still at the mercy of the weather, able only to get a little more advance warning than in the past. The weather answers only to God. Rain and hail will fall where they want to; freezing cold is totally inconsiderate of something as important as a Hokie football game.

We stand mute before the awesome power of the weather, but we should be even more awestruck at the power of the one who controls it, a power beyond our imagining. Neither, however, can we imagine the depths of God's love for us, a love that drove him to die on a cross for us.

All I remember was it was bitterly cold.
-- UVA head coach George Welsh on the 1982 Tech-UVa game

The power of the one who controls the weather is
beyond anything we can imagine,
but so is his love for us.

NOT WHAT THEY SEEM

Read Habakkuk 1:2-11.

"Why do you make me look at injustice? Why do you tolerate wrong? Destruction and violence are before me; there is strife, and conflict abounds" (v. 3).

Michael Vick rolled left, evaded the pressure, and headed downfield for a 75-yard touchdown run. Just another perfectly executed play, right? Not at all; it was, in fact, a totally botched play.

The Hokies were 9-0 and were headed toward the BCS title game when they met Temple on Nov. 20, 1999, and won easily 62-7. What happened early in the third quarter of that game provided a clear indication of just how special this whole season was.

Offensive coordinator Rickey Bustle sent down a play from the press box to assistant head coach Billy Hite on the sideline. Hite relayed the call to backup quarterback Grant Noel to signal in the play to Vick. That's when everything fell apart. Suddenly, Noel shouted back at Hite, who answered with a confused question. Frank Beamer noticed the commotion and asked if they needed a time out. By then, though, Vick had the play under way.

Why all the confusion? It seems Vick had left his wristband with its play-calling card inserted under plastic in the locker room at halftime. He thus borrowed Noel's, which turned out to be a big problem. Vick is left-handed; Noel is right-handed. That meant Bustle wrote Vick's plays to the opposite side of Noel's cards. Noel was shouting that Vick had to roll his wristband over.

Thus, Vick took the snap, turned for a play fake, and found himself alarmingly alone. Everybody else had gone in the opposite direction. "It was supposed to be a play fake to the right," Bustle said. "Michael went left. I look down and wonder, 'What the heck is he doing now?'"

Seventy-five yards later, he was scoring a touchdown on what appeared to be a brilliantly called and executed play.

Just like in football, sometimes in life things aren't what they seem. In our violent and convulsive times, we must confront the possibility of a new reality: that we are helpless in the face of anarchy; that injustice, destruction, and violence are pandemic in and symptomatic of our modern age. It seems that anarchy is winning, that the system of standards, values, and institutions we have cherished is crumbling while we watch.

But we should not be deceived or disheartened. God is in fact the arch-enemy of chaos, the creator of order and goodness and the architect of all of history. God is in control. We often misinterpret history as the record of mankind's accomplishments -- which it isn't -- rather than the unfolding of God's plan -- which it is. That plan has a clearly defined end: God will make everything right. In that day things will be what they seem.

Unlike any other business in the United States, sports must preserve an illusion of perfect innocence.
-- Author Lewis H. Lapham

**The forces of good and decency often seem
helpless before evil's power, but don't be fooled:
God is in control and will set things right.**

THE RIGHT MAN

Read Matthew 26:47-50; 27:1-10.

"The betrayer had arranged a signal with them: 'The one I kiss is the man; arrest him.' Going at once to Jesus, Judas said, 'Greetings, Rabbi!' and kissed him" (vv. 48-49).

Tech needed someone to "put fire in the eyes of the defeated and fear in the hearts of the weak." In other words, the Hokies needed a coach who could straighten out the football program. They found the right man for the job in Frank O'Rear Moseley.

World War II numbered among its casualties the Virginia Tech football program. After losing their coach, Jimmy Kitts, to the service, the Hokies fielded a team in 1942 of "overachieving smart kids who wanted to play." They surprised everyone by going 7-2-1 and beating Virginia 20-6. After that, though, Tech closed down its football program for two years.

The school revived football in 1945, but the war's effects in Blacksburg lingered long after young athletes flooded onto college campuses to take advantage of the GI Bill. Most of the veterans had had more than their share of military service and thus wanted nothing to do with Tech's cadet corps. "They just didn't get the players anymore," said UVa head coach Art Guepe. The program reached its nadir with a winless season in 1950 that included a 54-0 loss to William & Mary.

The athletic council went looking for a new coach and found Moseley, who had played with and roomed with Bear Bryant

at Alabama and was working as a Bryant assistant at Kentucky. After one four-hour interview, the council offered Moseley the longest and most lucrative contract ever for a Tech coach.

Their confidence was not misplaced. Moseley understood the desperation of the situation into which he was stepping, but he boldly announced Tech would have a winning season within five years. It took him only four; the Hokies went 8-0-1 in 1954.

Frank Moseley was the right man for the job.

What do you want to be when you grow up? Somehow you are supposed to know the answer to that question when you're a teenager, the time in life when common sense and logic are at their lowest ebb. Long after those halcyon teen years are left behind, you may make frequent career changes. You chase the job that gives you not just financial rewards but also some personal satisfaction and sense of accomplishment. You desire a profession that uses your abilities, that you enjoy doing, and that gives you a sense of contributing to something bigger than yourself.

God, too, wants you in the right job, one that he has designed specifically for you. After all, even Judas was the right man for what God needed done. To do his work, God gave you abilities, talents, and passions. Do what you do best and what you love -- just do it for God.

Frank Moseley came to Blacksburg armed with the verve that would carry the program from winless misery to the age of big-time athletics.
-- Doug Doughty and Roland Lazenby in 'Hoos 'n' Hokies

God has a job for you, one for which he gave you particular talents, abilities, and passions.

DAY 91

A GOOD IMPRESSION

Read John 1:1-18.

"In the beginning was the Word, and the Word was with God, and the Word was God. . . . The Word became flesh and made his dwelling among us" (vv. 1, 14).

One of the most valuable men in the history of contemporary Virginia Tech football didn't make a very good first impression on the men who would hire him.

Frank Beamer takes care of everything on the football field. Everything else to do with Hokie football is the purview of Dr. John Ballein, the school's associate director of athletics for football operations. An executive with Nike's football camp operations once called Ballein "the best in the country."

Back in 1987, though, Ballein was a recent college graduate looking for a coaching job. He sent out one hundred videotapes highlighting his virtues and talents. "I didn't know anybody," he said, "so I had to make myself different." He did that all right by making what was perhaps an unfortunate choice. The video featured a picture of Ballein from his college playing days complete with a mohawk haircut

Ron Zook, then a Tech assistant, saw the tape and showed it to assistant coach Billy Hite, who was not at all impressed. In fact, about the kindest thing Hite said was his questioning of Ballein's sexual preference. Impressed, though, by Ballein's gumption, Zook showed the tape to Beamer, who, as writer Chris Colston

put it, "figured Ballein was a few clowns shy of a circus." "I'm not too sure about this guy," Beamer said diplomatically.

But the persistent Zook convinced Beamer to give the hirsutely challenged physical education major a chance as a Tech graduate assistant. Except for 1988 when he coached at Western Kentucky, Ballein has been in Blacksburg ever since, his lasting impression much more favorable than his first one.

That guy in the apartment next door. A job search complete with interview. A twenty-year class reunion. The new neighbors. We are constantly about the fraught task of wanting to make an impression on people. We want them to remember us, obviously in a flattering way, which means we perhaps should be more careful about our haircuts than John Ballein was.

Even with instant communication on the Internet – perhaps especially with the Internet – we primarily influence the opinion others have of us by our words. After that, we can advance to the next level by making an impression with our actions.

God gave us an impression of himself in exactly the same way. In Jesus, God took the unprecedented step of appearing to mortals as one of us, as mere flesh and bone. We now know for all time the sorts of things God does and the sorts of things God says. In Jesus, God put his divine foot forward to make a good impression on each one of us.

I'm a pretty good judge of character, but I was wrong that time.
-- Frank Beamer on Dr. John Ballein

Through Jesus' words and actions,
God seeks to impress us with his love.

THE FAME GAME

Read 1 Kings 10:1-10, 18-29.

"King Solomon was greater in riches and wisdom than all the other kings of the earth. The whole world sought audience with Solomon" (vv. 23-24).

With one of the most unusual scoring plays in Tech football history, Matt Reidy was suddenly -- and briefly -- famous.

In 2009, Reidy was a senior lineback-rover who had earned a scholarship in 2008 primarily because of his excellence on special teams. On Sept. 26, the 11th-ranked Hokies humbled 9th-ranked Miami 31-7 in what was called "a total rear-end kicking in all phases of the game." One of the game's most exciting plays came when Reidy scored the lone touchdown of his college career with a one-of-a-kind punt return.

The Hokies led 14-0 when sophomore cornerback Jacob Sykes blocked a Hurricane punt. Reidy hurried toward the ball but stood idly by while teammate Marcus Davis tried to recover the slippery ball on a wet field. Finally, Reidy picked the ball up and "sashayed all of 3 feet into the end zone" in what "may have been the easiest, room-service TD in gridiron history."

It was a one yard punt return.

"I actually turned around to block for [Davis], because I thought he was going to get it," Reidy said. "I saw him slipping around so I said I might as well pick it up." He did, and the unusual way he scored brought Reidy unexpected fame among media members

and fans and some ribbing from his teammates. "Reidy just said he's not going to hang out with us anymore now that he knows what the end zone is like," quipped linebacker Cody Grimm.

"I never thought I would score in college," Reidy confessed, but he did, and he was famous for it.

Have you ever wanted to be famous? Hanging out with other rich and famous people, having folks with microphones listen to what you say, throwing money around like toilet paper, meeting adoring and clamoring fans, signing autographs, and posing for the paparazzi before you climb into your imported sports car?

Many of us yearn to be famous, well-known in the places and by the people that we believe matter. That's all fame amounts to: strangers knowing your name and your face.

The truth is that you are already famous where it really does matter, which excludes TV's talking heads, screaming teenagers, rapt moviegoers, or D.C. power brokers. You are famous because Almighty God knows your name, your face, and everything else there is to know about you.

If a persistent photographer snapped you pondering this fame – the only kind that has eternal significance – would the picture show the world unbridled joy or the shell-shocked expression of a mug shot?

When you play a sport, you have two things in mind. One is to get into the Hall of Fame and the other is to go to heaven when you die.
– Lee Trevino

You're already famous because God knows
your name and your face,
which may be either reassuring or terrifying.

YOU NEVER KNOW

Read Exodus 3:1-12.

*"But Moses said to God, 'Who am I, that I should go to
Pharaoh and bring the Israelites out of Egypt?' And God
said, 'I will be with you'" (vv. 11-12a).*

Bruce Arians' football career at Tech had been such a disaster
that he was looking for a junior high school coaching job rather
than come back for a fifth year. Then he got a call from the head
coach and almost overnight became both the starting quarterback
and the team captain.

During the evening of Jan. 3, 1974, Hokie head coach Charlie
Coffey decided to resign. He left town the next morning. Athletic
director Frank Moseley brought in Alabama offensive coordinator
Jimmy Sharpe, who brought with him the Wishbone offense the
Tide was then running so successfully. Sharpe had a big problem,
though: He didn't have a quarterback to run the thing. The only
experienced quarterback on his roster was Arians.

But Arians was a problem, too. He had become so discouraged
with Coffey and the program that he had begun looking for a job
as a junior high coach rather than return. Still, he was Sharpe's
best and last hope. Assistant coach Terry Don Phillips ran Arians
down and talked him into meeting with Sharpe. The head coach
was brief and to the point; he told Arians, "Come on out for spring
and, if you can't make it, I'll get you a high-school job." "I've got
nothing to lose but twenty pounds," Arians replied.

Two weeks later he returned to the coach's office and asked him what the deal was. Sharpe's reply? "You're the captain of the team. You're the starting quarterback. You'll start all eleven games unless you break a leg."

Arians did and he didn't. The fifth-year senior who just knew his college playing days were over threw for 952 yards and three touchdowns and had eight touchdowns rushing.

You never know what you can do you until -- like Bruce Arians -- you get a chance to do something you didn't expect -- or until – like Moses -- you have to. Serving in the military, maybe even in combat. Standing by a friend while everyone else excoriates her. Undergoing agonizing medical treatment and managing to smile. You never know what life will demand of you.

It's that way too in your relationship with God. As Moses discovered, you never know where or when God will call you or what God will ask of you. You do know that God expects you to be faithful and willing to trust him even when he calls you to tasks that daunt and dismay you.

You can respond faithfully to whatever God calls you to do for him. That's because even though you never know what lies ahead, you do know that God will both lead you and provide what you need.

There's one word to describe baseball: You never know.
– Yogi Berra

You never know what God will ask you to do,
but you always know he will provide everything
you need to do it.

HURRY UP AND WAIT

Read Acts 1:1-14.

"Do not leave Jerusalem, but wait for the gift my Father promised, which you have heard me speak about" (v. 4).

The anxious waiting stretched out for so long that Katie Ollendick finally got enough and went back to her hotel room.

On March 14, 1998, the Virginia Tech senior competed in the high-jump competition at the NCAA Track and Field Championships in Indianapolis. Ollendick cleared the bar at 5 feet, 10 inches, which left her twelfth in the competition. She knew she wouldn't win, but one of her primary goals was to finish high enough to make All-America. That hinged on whether or not she had placed among the top eight American-born competitors.

"When it was all over, it looked like I was going to be the No. 8 or No. 9 American," Ollendick said. "I was right on the borderline." So Ollendick and her parents; Lori Taylor, the Tech women's track coach; and assistant coach Roosevelt Lofton waited for the All-America certification list to be posted. And they waited.

Finally, the coaches sent Ollendick and her family back to the hotel so she could take a shower and relax while the coaches waited and figured. "We knew for sure there were three girls who were non-Americans," Taylor said. Since Ollendick had finished twelfth, there had to be four. "I wouldn't say we were doubtful, but we weren't certainly expecting it would happen."

When the All-America list was finally posted, Ollendick was

No. 8, thus becoming the first Virginia Tech women's track and field athlete to earn All-American status since distance runner Maggie Lasaga in 1987.

An ecstatic Taylor and Lofton weren't ready to end Ollendick's anxious wait. They forced her to endure one "pretty dirty trick" by telling her she was ninth before they broke out in laughter and told her the truth, ending the wait and beginning the celebration.

You rush to your doctor's appointment and wind up sitting in the appropriately named waiting room for an hour. You wait in the concessions line at a Hokie game. You're put on hold when you call a tragically misnamed "customer service" center. All of that waiting is time in which we seem to do nothing but feel the precious minutes of our life ticking away.

Sometimes we even wait for God. We have needs, and we desperately call upon the Lord and are disappointed when we perhaps get no immediate answer.

But Jesus' last command to his disciples was to wait. Moreover, the entire of our Christian life is spent in an attitude of waiting for Jesus' return. While we wait for God, we hold steadfast to his promises, we continue our ministry, we remain in communion with him through prayer and devotion.

In other words, we don't just wait; we grow stronger in our faith. Waiting for God is never time lost.

An agonizing wait. A horrible wait.
-- Katie Ollendick and coach Lori Taylor on their day at Indianapolis

Since God acts on his time and not ours,
we often must wait for him,
using the time to strengthen our faith.

STAR POWER

Read Luke 10:1-3, 17-20.

"The Lord appointed seventy-two others and sent them two by two ahead of him to every town and place where he was about to go" (v. 1).

Russell McCubbin was never a star wearing the maroon and orange, but he did quite well on the streets of Hollywood.

A highly recruited football and track star out of high school, McCubbin never even lettered as a Tech football player, though he was on the team in 1953 and '54. On the freshman squad in '53, he played opposite a Duke guard touted as an All-America and "beat [him] all over the field." During the game, McCubbin looked across at the guard and said, "Son, if you're All-American, then what do you think I ought to be?"

After the 1954 season, McCubbin enlisted in the Army, served for three years, and then returned to Blacksburg briefly in 1957. But, he said, "I realized that I had lost my desire to play, and I got the wanderlust." Legend has it that McCubbin walked off the field during a tough practice. "Hey, McCubbin! Where you goin'?" head coach Frank Moseley called after him. "Coach," he replied, "I'm goin' to Hollywood." McCubbin always denied that the story was true.

Be that as it may, he did go to Hollywood, hitchhiking to Los Angeles where he pestered agents in the day and parked cars at night. One of his early breaks came as a member of a photo spread

in *Life* magazine. He was one of fifteen half-naked men hanging out in a tree, all aiming at becoming the next Tarzan. McCubbin didn't get the part.

He did land plenty of parts, though, in what turned out to be a 34-year Hollywood career. He had roles in more than 190 films, TV shows, and plays. He acted with John Wayne, Clint Eastwood, Gary Cooper, and Clark Gable, among others.

Football teams are like other organizations in that they may have a star but the star would be nothing without the supporting cast as Russ McCubbin showed with his career. It's the same in a company, in a government bureaucracy, in a military unit, and just about any other team of people with a common goal.

That includes the team known as a church. It may have its "star" in the preacher, who is – like the quarterback or the company CEO – the most visible representative of the team. Preachers are, after all, God's paid, trained professionals.

But when Jesus assembled a team of seventy-two folks, he didn't have anybody on the payroll or any seminary graduates. All he had were no-names who loved him. And nothing has changed. God's church still depends on those whose only pay is the satisfaction of serving and whose only qualification is their love for God. God's church needs you.

You may have the greatest bunch of individual stars in the world, but if they don't play together, the club won't be worth a dime.

– Babe Ruth

**Yes, the church needs its professional clergy,
but it also needs those who serve as volunteers
because they love God; the church needs you.**

STRANGE BUT TRUE

Read Isaiah 9:2-7.

"The zeal of the Lord Almighty will accomplish this" (v. 7).

Strange but true: Tech running back Mike Imoh officially set a school record a day after the game was over.

As a sophomore in 2003, Imoh became the first Hokie to return a kickoff for a touchdown since 1992 when he went 91 yards in the 47-13 smashing of Connecticut. He led the Big East in kick returns that season and had the third-best average in the nation.

On Nov. 6, 2004, the Hokies played UNC and turned the game over to their junior tailback. He got the ball seven straight times on Tech's first possession, had more than 100 yards by halftime, and broke off a 47-yard romp on his first carry of the last half. "It would have been nice to take it to the house," Imoh said.

Imoh scored two touchdowns, caught one pass, and returned three kickoffs for 48 yards as Tech edged the Heels 27-24 on its way to the ACC title. He finished with 236 yards on 31 carries and received some ribbing from teammates, who let him know he had finished five yards short of the school record, set the year before by Kevin Jones. Imoh even called Jones and told him he had just missed his record. Sunday morning, though, running backs coach Billy Hite told Imoh he'd better call Jones again.

Carter Myers, the statistician for the Tech radio crew, realized that his figures didn't match the official game stats. So that night,

he turned on his video recorder and reviewed every play. He discovered that one of Imoh's carries had been credited to another back. Officials from Tech's sports information office notified their counterparts in Chapel Hill; after checking, they confirmed the mistake and made the change in the official game records.

A day after the game was over, Imoh now had 243 yards on 32 carries, a new school record.

Life is just strange, isn't it? How else to explain the college bowl situation, Dr. Phil, tattoos, curling, tofu, and teenagers? Isn't it strange that today we have more ways to stay in touch with each other yet are losing the intimacy of personal contact?

And how strange is God's plan to save us? Think a minute about what God did. He could have come roaring down, destroying and blasting everyone whose sinfulness offended him, which, of course, is pretty much all of us. Then he could have brushed off his hands, nodded the divine head, and left a scorched planet in his wake. All in a day's work.

Instead, God came up with a totally novel plan: He would save the world by becoming a human being, letting himself be humiliated, tortured, and killed, and thus establishing a kingdom of justice and righteousness that will last forever.

It's a strange way to save the world – but it's true.

It may sound strange, but many champions are made champions by setbacks.

-- Olympic champion Bob Richards

**It's strange but true: God allowed himself
to be killed on a cross to save the world.**

DAY 97

CELEBRATION TIME

Read Luke 15:1-10.

"There is rejoicing in the presence of the angels of God over one sinner who repents" (v. 10).

The fans were still celebrating even after the Hokies had a post-game team meeting, so they went out and crashed the party.

On Feb. 1, 1986, Tech hosted Memphis State in a Metro Conference showdown. The Tigers were ranked No. 2 in the nation and expected to move into the top slot with a win. The Hokies were no slouches; they were ranked 16th, would finish the season at 22-9, and would land in the NCAA Tournament. Only five days before, though, the Tigers had drilled Tech 83-61 in Memphis.

Students camped out to get tickets, and Cassell Coliseum was packed. All-American guard Dell Curry said, "It was just an electric atmosphere from start to finish."

With a little more than three minutes left to play, Tech led by four, but the Hokies had had a 10-point lead only a short time before, so the Tigers were on a run. Head coach Charlie Moir said, "Someone had to step up, and Dell did." Curry fired one of his long-range bombs; it didn't matter how far he was from the basket. As one writer put it, "His range was pretty much anywhere in the arena." Curry nailed the shot, just another big one in a game full of them; he finished with 28 points and nine rebounds.

After that, sophomore center Roy Brow hit a late jumper, Iowa transfer Johnny Fort hit three free throws, and Tech claimed a

76-72 win, touching off a wild, zany, and prolonged celebration.

The Hokies held their usual postgame team meeting and then discovered that their ecstatic fans were hanging around still going quite nuts. So the players went back out to celebrate with them. "That was great to see them still out there that long after the game," Curry said.

The Hokies just won another game. You got that new job or that promotion. You just held your newborn child in your arms. Life has those grand moments that call for celebration. You may jump up and down and scream in a wild frenzy at Lane Stadium or share a sedate candlelight dinner at home -- but you celebrate.

Consider then a celebration that is actually beyond our wildest imagining, one that fills every niche and corner of the very home of God and the angels. Imagine a celebration in Heaven, which also has its grand moments.

They are touched off when someone comes to faith in Jesus. Heaven itself rings with the joyous sounds of the singing and dancing of the celebrating angels. Even God rejoices when just one person – you or someone you have introduced to Christ -- turns to him.

When you said "yes" to Christ, you made the angels dance.

The place didn't go berserk. It just stayed that way.
-- The Hokie Huddler *on the atmosphere in Cassell Coliseum for the*
1986 Memphis State game

God himself joins the angels in heavenly
celebration when even a single person
turns to him through faith in Jesus.

JUST PERFECT

Read Matthew 5:43-48.

"Be perfect, therefore, as your heavenly Father is perfect"
(v. 48).

Strictly speaking, "perfect" is not an adjective that can be applied to a day in our lives with complete correctness. If ever Frank Beamer had a day that could be called "perfect," though, it was Nov. 9, 1968.

Beamer, of course, is most famous as Tech's legendary head football coach. Years before he coached the maroon and orange, however, he wore the colors as a player, an undersized cornerback teammate Mike Widger called a "tough son of a gun" who "did things on the field that a 5 feet, 10 inch cornerback shouldn't do."

Beamer was a three-year starter from 1966-68 who once said he had a fondness for players who were like him -- that is, they valued hard work -- but that he liked for them "to be a lot bigger and a lot faster than I was." Beamer has said he had "that football sense" that enabled him to "get myself to the right place at the right time." He did just that on that "perfect" day in 1968.

Back then, a win over Richmond wasn't a sure thing. In fact, the Spiders finished the 1968 season ranked 18th in the nation. So no one was surprised when the game was still up for grabs in the third quarter. With 8:54 left, Beamer stepped in front of a Spider pass and maneuvered his way through the snow and the wind across 50 yards of turf into the end zone. Tech went on to win

31-18. Beamer did double duty as the team's holder and completed a 9-yard pass on a fake field goal.

Could the day get any better? For Frank Beamer it did. That evening he had a blind date with a young woman named Cheryl Oakley. Today, Hokie fans the world over know her as Cheryl Beamer. Overall, it was pretty much a perfect day.

Nobody's perfect; we make mistakes every day, thus rendering each of our days imperfect. To insist upon personal or professional perfection in our lives is to establish an impossibly high standard that will eventually destroy us physically, emotionally, and mentally.

Yet that is exactly the standard God sets for us. Our love is to be perfect, never ceasing, never failing, never qualified – just the way God loves us. And Jesus didn't limit his command to only preachers and goody-two-shoes types. All of his disciples are to be perfect as they navigate their way through the world's ambiguous definition and understanding of love.

But that's impossible! Well, not necessarily if to love perfectly is to serve God wholeheartedly and to follow Jesus with single-minded devotion. Anyhow, in his perfect love for us, God makes allowance for our imperfect love and the consequences of it in the perfection of Jesus.

Practice does not make you perfect as nobody is perfect, but it does make you better.
-- Soccer coach Adrian Parrish

In his perfect love for us, God provides a way for us to escape the consequences of our imperfect love for him: Jesus.

DAY 99

RESPECTFULLY YOURS

Read Mark 8:31-38.

"He then began to teach them that the Son of Man must suffer many things and be rejected by the elders, chief priests and teachers of the law, and that he must be killed" (v. 31).

Tech was 6-1; UVa was only 2-3 and was coming off a last-minute loss to Clemson. It was the Hokies, though, who didn't get any respect heading into their showdown on Oct. 18, 1980.

Some of the disrespect resulted from the immediate past results of the series; Tech hadn't beaten the Cavaliers since 1976. Most of the skepticism surrounding Tech's football team was engendered, however, by the Hokies' weak schedule. Four of the wins had come against teams that would eventually be classified as Division 1-AA: East Tennessee State, William and Mary, James Madison, and Rhode Island.

As the season unwound, though, the Tech players grew progressively more irritated at the constant denigration of the team. "People talk about our schedule and they don't know what kind of team we have," said quarterback Steve Casey. "They haven't seen us and they didn't think we could beat Virginia."

So the Hokies had something to prove, and prove it they did. They blasted Virginia 30-0, the widest margin of victory in the series since a 40-6 win over the Cavs in 1960. Third-year head coach Bill Dooley, who would whip Virginia six times in his nine

seasons at the helm, took advantage of rainy weather to turn tail-back Cyrus Lawrence loose. The sophomore, who would become the school's all-time leading rusher with 3,767 yards, set a school record with 40 carries. His 194 yards and two touchdowns paced a ground game that rolled up 295 yards. The Tech defense, meanwhile, never let Virginia past the Hokie 27.

The team nobody respected until that day finished the regular season 8-3 and played in the Peach Bowl.

Rodney Dangerfield made a good living as a comedian with a repertoire that was basically only countless variations on one punch line: "I don't get no respect." Dangerfield was successful because he struck a chord with his audience. No one wants to play football for a program that no one respects. You want the respect, the esteem, and the regard that you feel you've earned.

But more often than not, you don't get it. Still, you shouldn't feel too badly; you're in good company. In the ultimate example of disrespect, Jesus – the very Son of God -- was treated as the worst type of criminal. He was arrested, bound, scorned, ridiculed, spit upon, tortured, condemned, and executed.

God allowed his son to undergo such treatment because of his high regard and his love for you. You are respected by almighty God! Could anyone else's respect really matter?

I've never seen a team that wanted to win a game so much.
-- Tech quarterback Steve Casey on the 1980 Virginia game

You may not get the respect you deserve,
but at least nobody's spitting on you
and driving nails into you as they did to Jesus.

THE END

Read Revelation 22:1-17.

"I am the Alpha and the Omega, the First and the Last, the Beginning and the End" (v. 13).

Johnny Oates knew his life was nearing its end even if it was way too soon. That knowledge let him turn each day he had left into a blessing.

On May 4, 2002, Oates became the first person in Virginia Tech baseball history to have his jersey retired. Before a doubleheader at English Field, he was honored in a ceremony that included the unveiling on the outfield fence of his name and old number (15). "To realize there's only one circle out there, it's pretty special," Oates said.

The October before, Oates, who was only 56, was diagnosed with a particularly nasty form of brain cancer. Doctors gave him fourteen months to live. "I'm going to show 'em," Oates responded. "It's going to be longer than 14 months."

A catcher who is in the Virginia Tech Sports Hall of Fame, Oates attended Tech from 1964-67 before turning pro. He hit .410 as a sophomore and .342 as a junior. After being drafted by the Baltimore Orioles, he made it to the majors, playing with five teams from 1970-81. He managed the Orioles from 1991-94.

In recalling his time at Tech, Oates said he always felt that head football coach Jerry Claiborne was upset with him that he didn't play football. He did spend time with the football team once --

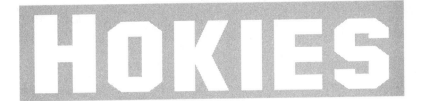

when baseball coach Red Laird sent him to the football team's winter workouts to lose weight. "I lost my weight quick," he said, "because I never wanted to go back to that football training."

Oates once said, "When you look at it, it's a blessing" about his cancer because it gave him precious time to focus on what mattered the most to him -- his family. Johnny Oates died on Dec. 24, 2004, more than three years after the original diagnosis. As he had said he would, he made it longer than fourteen months.

Everything ends. The very stars in the heavens have a life cycle, though admittedly it's rather lengthy. Erosion eventually will wear a boulder to a pebble. Life itself is temporary; all living things have a beginning and an end.

Within the framework of our individual lifetimes, we meet endings. Loved ones, friends, and pets die; relationships fracture; jobs dry up; our health, clothes, lawn mowers, TV sets – they all wear out. Even this world as we know it will end.

But one of the greatest ironies of God's gift of life is that not even death is immune from the great truth of creation that all things must end. That's because through Jesus' life, death, and resurrection, God himself acted to end any power death once had over life. In other words, because of Jesus, the end of life has ended. Eternity is ours for the claiming.

No, no, no, no, no. I'm totally at peace. In my life, God's already done a miracle, the fact that I feel so at peace.
-- Johnny Oates when asked if he felt he'd been handed a raw deal

**Everything ends;
thanks to Jesus Christ, so does death.**

NOTES
(by Devotion Day Number)

1 A few of the cadets would gather . . . about as level as a side of Brush Mountain.": Chris Colston, *Virginia Tech Football Vault: The History of the Hokies* (Atlanta: Whitman Publishing, LLC, 2009), p. 7.

1 They had to use lots of persuasion . . . everybody wanted to play on the first team or none.: Colston, *Virginia Tech Football Vault*, p. 7.

2 Some disappointed Tech fans were already filing toward the Lane Stadium exits: Randy King, "Hokies Shuck Huskers' Upset Bid," *The Roanoke Times*, Sept. 20, 2009.

2 "always a chance when . . . wanted to give him a ball he could catch,": King, "Hokies Shuck Huskers' Upset Bid."

2 Coale thought he had scored,: King, "Hokies Shuck Huskers' Upset Bid."

2 Oh, my goodness gracious!: King, "Hokies Shuck Huskers' Upset Bid."

3 Since Wiley persistently had a problem with the heat,: Doug Doughty and Roland Lazenby, *'Hoos 'N' Hokies The Rivalry: 100 Years of Virginia/Virginia Tech Football* (Dallas: Taylor Publishing Company, 1995), p. 148.

3 "sitting in the corner, soaking in ice, . . . come together to make something happen.": Doughty and Lazenby, p. 151.

3 Coach Dooley raised our ire enough to go out and make a run of it again in the second half.: Doughty and Lazenby, p. 151.

4 She began wearing a prosthetic . . . that she described as "normal.": "Tennis Phenom J.J. Larson Does Things Just Like Everyone Else," *redOrbit.com*, June 10, 2005, http://www.redorbit.com/news/health/155160, Dec. 8, 2010.

4 When she was nine, her dad put . . . forefinger of her prosthesis and tossing it.: Jimmy Robertson, "Tennis Team hopes to Ace Competition with Its Unique Freshman Star," *Virginia Tech Magazine*, Spring 2005, http://www.vtmagazine.vt.edu/spring05/sports.html, Dec. 7, 2010.

4 a serve clocked at almost 100 miles per hour. . . . whipping it off with her right hand: Thomas Emerick, "Larson Overcomes Setbacks to Enjoy Success," *CollegiateTimes.com*, April 4, 2008, http://www.collegiatetimes.com/stories/11099, Dec. 8, 2010.

4 She never uses her arm . . . on her teammates and her coaching staff.: Emerick.

5 When Frank Beamer was 7, . . . as badly as he was burned.": Roland Lazenby, "Tempered Steel: How Frank Beamer Got That Way," *The Roanoker*, Dec. 15, 2010, http://theroanoker.com/interests/tempered-steel-how-frank-beamer-got-that-way-2010, Dec. 20, 2010.

5 It was a hard time for all of us, but we made it.: Lazenby, "Tempered Steel."

6 "never run more than 100 yards in [his] life,": Mark Schlabach, *What It Means to Be a Hokie* (Chicago: Triumph Books, 2006), p. 87.

6 As a junior in 1965, Stafford . . . and found me still on the road.": Schlabach, p. 87.

6 At that point, his teammates stretched a piece of twine across the highway close to Salem and used it as a finish line.: Schlabach, pp. 87-88.

6 Even after he spent a couple of hours . . . the coach "got a kick out of it.": Schlabach, p. 88.

6 I still have that finish line to this day.: Schlabach, p. 88.

7 The closer who led the country in saves: Mark Berman, "Hokies Break Through," *The Roanoke Times*, April 19, 2010.

7 He told him to relax, but he was really stalling to slow down the Cav pitcher's momentum.: Berman, "Hokies Break Through."

8 "unbelievably decisive spanking": Randy King, "Turning on the Juice," *The Roanoke Times*, Oct. 17, 1999.

8 the largest shutout defeat of a ranked team . . . was cooked and done by halftime.": King, "Turning on the Juice."

8 "I believe this is a special night in Blacksburg,": King, "Turning on the Juice."

8 Wouldn't you be embarrassed? Of course it's embarrassing.: King, "Turning on the Juice."

9 "one of the most versatile and talented players to ever sign with the Hokies.": Schlabach, p. 179.

9 when head coach Jimmy Sharpe was fired . . . crumbles and it would set us back light-years.": Schlabach, p. 178.

9 "That was really a devastating time for us," . . . gave Fitzgerald and his brother structure: Schlabach, p. 175.

9 Fitzgerald learned an indelible lesson from . . . you'll do it for someone else.": Schlabach, p. 174.

9 "has made a habit of giving all he's got.": "Filling the Need," *Virginia Tech Magazine*, Spring 2008, http://www.vtmagazine.edu/spring08/shorts.html, Jan. 6, 2011.

10 Carlos Dixon dreamed of playing basketball . . . Virginia Tech showed the most interest.: Mike Harris, *Game of My Life: Virginia Tech* (Champaign, IL: Sports Publishing L.L.C., 2006), p. 220.

10 That latter news changed everything . . . it would all work out in the end.: Harris, *Game of My Life* p. 221.

10   his senior "was just terrific on both ends" of the court.: Harris, *Game of My Life*, p. 225.

10   That was his dream; he always wanted to play in the ACC.: Harris, *Game of My Life*, p. 226.

11   "the consummate southern gentleman off the field.": Chris Colston, *Tales from the Virginia Tech Sideline* (Champaign, IL: Sports Publishing L.L.C., 2007), p. 55.

11   After the game, Beamer . . . to be illegal.: Colston, *Tales from the Virginia Tech Sideline*, p. 54.

11   The Tuesday after the game, . . . the lollipop in the coach's chair.: Colston, *Tales from the Virginia Tech Sideline*, pp. 54-55.

11   When Beamer arrived, he pulled out . . . to hit that golf ball straight. . . . : Colston, *Tales from the Virginia Tech Sideline*, p. 55.

11   Later that day, someone asked, . . . that said, 'THIS way.'": Colston, *Tales from the Virginia Tech Sideline*, p. 55.

11   The stuff that worries many coaches doesn't bother [Frank] Beamer.: Colston, *Tales from the Virginia Tech Sideline*, p. 54.

12   as quarterback Tyrod Taylor started scrambling . . . escorted Nosal into the locker room.: Michael Klopman, "Greg Nosal, Virginia Tech Left Guard, Loses FINGER Tip During Game," *The Huffington Post*, Oct. 11, 2010, http://www.huffingtonpost.com/2010/10/11/greg-nosal-loses-finger_n_758524.html, Nov. 10, 2010.

12   lost a half inch of the end of his finger. . . . finally located in Nosal's glove.: Tyler Reisinger, "Virginia Tech Lineman Severs Pinkie Finger," *Sportsgrid.com*, Oct. 12, 2010, http://www.sportsgrid.com/ncaa-football/virginia-tech-lineman-severs-pinkie-finger, Nov. 10, 2010.

12   Team surgeon Marc Seigal said the . . . when Tech had a secure 31-7 lead: Klopman.

12   I guess it's a big deal if your pinkie got ripped off.: Klopman.

13   "a wobby, rainbow pass that "settled in the nervous hands of Garnell Wilds.": Randy King, "Uncalled Trickery a Treat for Hokies." *The Roanoke Times*, Sept 30, 2001.

13   Tech had worked on a fake-punt . . . end zone then right on home.": King, "Uncalled Trickery a Treat for Hokies."

13   That's why you recruit good players; sometimes they can overcome coaching.: King, "Uncalled Trickery a Treat for Hokies."

14   "Dave is such a hard worker," . . . doing something to get better.": Randy King, "No Longer a String Bean," *The Roanoke Times*, Aug. 25, 2000.

14   "I lived by the rule: force feed . . . I just inhaled food.": King, "No Longer a String Bean."

15   Have a little fun and maybe last the full seven innings before getting beat.: Mark Berman, "Angela Tincher Pitches No-Hitter," *The Roanoke Times*, March 28, 2008.

15   probably the most famous softball player . . . I guess I should run now.": Berman, "Angela Tincher Pitches No-Hitter."

15   Getting to play them was a great experience. And to win? Ridiculous.: Berman, "Angela Tincher Pitches No-Hitter."

16   Athletic officials were so excited and so sure . . . a new eight-year contract as coach and athletic director.: Doughty and Lazenby, p. 71.

16   two of the leaders of the Virginia Tech . . . headed in the right direction under Moseley.: Doughty and Lazenby, p. 72.

17   Harris "does everything for them,": Bill Hass, "Bill Hass on the ACC: Just Call Him Macho Harris and Watch Him Change a Game," *TheACC.com*, Dec. 3, 2008, http://www.theacc.com/sports/m-footbl/spec-rel/120308aaa.html, Aug. 5, 2010.

17   "I got it from my dad," . . . Nobody called me that.": Hass, "Bill Hass on the ACC: Just Call Him Macho Harris."

17   He wanted to name me a masculine name.: Hass, "Bill Hass on the ACC: Just Call Him Macho Harris."

18   "Hokies always felt a comradeship with . . . and Christmas five weeks early.": Colston, *Virginia Tech Football Vault*, p. 33.

18   The *Times* sent out society writers . . . through downtown Roanoke to the stadium.: Colston, *Virginia Tech Football Vault*, p. 35.

18   I'll always remember the VMI-VPI . . . got for a kid from Hillsville, Virginia.: Colston, *Virginia Tech Football Vault*, p. 35.

19   We have a stick-to-itiveness.": Mark Berman, "Hokies Get Last Gasp," *The Roanoke Times*, Jan. 29, 2010.

19   "Not many people are winning on the road in the ACC,": Berman, "Hokies Get Last Gasp."

19   "Everytime we huddled up, somebody said, 'We're still in it,'": Berman, "Hokies Get Last Gasp."

19   At that point, Greenberg ordered a full-court press.: Berman, "Hokies Get Last Gasp."

20   "the best option quarterback in the country,": Doughty and Lazenby, p. 181.

20   The Hokies wound up in the Independence . . . situation was soothed somewhat: Doughty and Lazenby, p. 184.

21   A youth named Floyd Meade was . . . he began to feed,: Chris Colston, *Tales from the Virginia Tech Sideline*, p. 2.

21   and train a turkey to gobble on command.: "From Gobbler to HokieBird," *About Virginia Tech*, http://www.vt.edu/about/hokie.html, Nov. 29, 2010.

21   Tech's original mascot introduced . . . the first game of the 1912 season.: Colston, *Tales from the Virginia Tech Sideline*, p. 2.

21   Meade dressed in a three-piece suit . . . pulled by the turkey.: Colston, *Virginia Tech Football Vault*, p. 15.

21   With one quite bizarre . . . reinforced the school's two nicknames:: Colston, *Tales from the Virginia Tech Sideline*, p. 14.

21   Gobblers, which had become . . . school athletics around 1908: Colston, *Virginia Tech Football Vault*, p. 14.

21   The school president declared pulling the cart . . . Meade ditched it after one game.: "From Gobbler to HokieBird."

21   He continued, however, to bring live mascots to games: Colston, *Virginia Tech Football Vault*, p. 15.

21   with each mascot winding up as the main course for dinner at season's end.: Colston, *Tales from the Virginia Tech Sideline*, p. 2.

21   He eventually passed the tradition on . . . until he retired in 1953.: Colston, *Virginia Tech Football Vault*, p. 15.

21   The first permanent costumed Gobbler showed up . . . Hokiebird costume first appeared in 1987.: "From Gobbler to HokieBird."

21   One story claimed the term "Gobbler" . . . athletes "gobbled" up their food servings.: "From Gobbler to HokieBird."

22   While West Virginia was going in . . . you can always pull it down and run.": Colston, *Tales from the Virginia Tech Sideline*, p. 73.

22   I'll tell you what I said. I said a prayer.: Colston, *Tales from the Virginia Tech Sideline*, p. 75.

23   "the greatest and saddest of Tech football stories.": Doughty and Lazenby, p. 88.

23   "the instincts, the fearlessness, and . . . to put the big chill on a ball carrier,": Doughty and Lazenby, p. 89.

23   Loria was so good he should gave gotten two letters: one for linebacker and one for safety.: Doughty and Lazenby, p. 89.

23   "That defense hurt people," . . . because he always knew what he was doing.": Doughty and Lazenby, p. 89.

23   No one knows when he is going . . . death might come in the blink of an eye.: Jim & Julie S. Bettinger, *The Book of Bowden* (Nashville: TowleHouse Publishing, 2001), p. 21.

24   Jullien grew up in Greece wrestling . . . if he'd like to join the Hokies.": Mark Berman, "Greek Thrower Gains Lofty Status," *The Roanoke Times*, June 9, 2003.

24   "I had no idea Virginia Tech existed before being contacted" by Jack,": Lindsay Pieper, "Va. Tech Title-Holder Trades Concertos for Championships," CBSSports.com, May 2, 2006, http://www.cstv.com/sports/c-track/uwire/050206aad.html, Jan. 17, 2011.

24   he figured he would give it a try . . . as a freshman at a college in northern Greece.: Berman, "Greek Thrower Gains Lofty Status."

24   Jullien started playing when he was 9 years old.: Pieper.

24   "My arms because too stiff . . . "I stopped the violin because of the hammer.": Berman, "Greek Thrower Gains Lofty Status."

25   "I remember going into the locker room, . . . thinking the season was going downhill,": Harris, *Game of My Life*, p. 164.

25   "I didn't actually give a talk," . . . going to get it done.'": Harris, *Game of My Life*, p. 163.

25   A lot of people think . . . a good leader, which is not true.: Harris, *Game of My Life*, p. 157.

25   "ambivalent, vacillating, impulsive, unsubmissive.": John MacArthur, *Twelve Ordinary Men* (Nashville: W Publishing Group, 2002), p. 39.

25   "the greatest preacher among the apostles" and the "dominant figure" in the birth of the church.: MacArthur, p. 39.

26   The Hokies "were cooked. . . . too good for us, that's for certain,": Randy King, "Quite the Surprise," *The Roanoke Times*, Sept. 21, 2008.

26   the second biggest comeback in Beamer's . . . "The boys like my dancing,": King, "Quite the Surprise."

26   Oh, my gosh, I've never seen Coach Beamer like that before.: Aaron McFarling, "Come-from-Behind Win Leaves Hokies Giddy," *The Roanoke Times*, Sept. 21, 2008.

27   Kinzer collapsed into a nervous wreck . . . "I couldn't believe how nervous I was,": Schlabach, p. 193.

27   When you're out there on the field, you're really not envrouse because you're so focused on what you're doing.: Schlabach, p. 193.

28   "the most important buzzer-beater in Virginia Tech history.": Jim Sumner, "Looking Back: Virginia Tech's Road to the 1973 NIT Title," TheACC.com, Feb. 28, 2009, http://www.theacc.com/sports/m-baskbl/spec-rel/021809aaa.html, Aug. 5, 2010.

28   "too small, too slow, and too Virginian" to win.: Sumner.

28   to find himself covered by all 6'3" of . . . wouldn't be able to see the basket,": Sumner.

29   "Blacksburg was a much better fit for me," . . . downtown easily or get to church.": Harris, p. 10.

29   he "was late to church, not sent." . . . "a great person, a great leader.": Harris, p. 16.

29   He was always going to class, . . . always had the Good Book with him.: Harris, p. 16.

30   who was playing his seventh season: Doughty and Lazenby, p. 21.

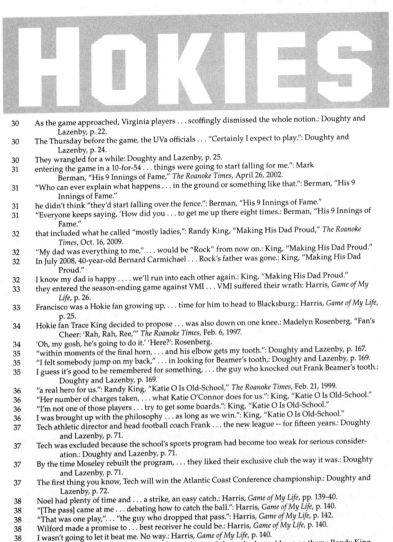

HOKIES

30   As the game approached, Virginia players . . . scoffingly dismissed the whole notion.: Doughty and Lazenby, p. 22.

30   The Thursday before the game, the UVa officials . . . "Certainly I expect to play.": Doughty and Lazenby, p. 24.

30   They wrangled for a while: Doughty and Lazenby, p. 25.

31   entering the game in a 10-for-54 . . . things were going to start falling for me.": Mark Berman, "His 9 Innings of Fame," *The Roanoke Times*, April 26, 2002.

31   "Who can ever explain what happens . . . in the ground or something like that.": Berman, "His 9 Innings of Fame."

31   he didn't think "they'd start falling over the fence.": Berman, "His 9 Innings of Fame."

31   "Everyone keeps saying, 'How did you . . . to get me up there eight times.: Berman, "His 9 Innings of Fame."

32   that included what he called "mostly ladies,": Randy King, "Making His Dad Proud," *The Roanoke Times*, Oct. 16, 2009.

32   "My dad was everything to me," . . . would be "Rock" from now on.: King, "Making His Dad Proud."

32   In July 2008, 40-year-old Bernard Carmichael . . . Rock's father was gone.: King, "Making His Dad Proud."

32   I know my dad is happy . . . . we'll run into each other again.: King, "Making His Dad Proud."

33   they entered the season-ending game against VMI . . . VMI suffered their wrath: Harris, *Game of My Life*, p. 26.

33   Francisco was a Hokie fan growing up, . . . time for him to head to Blacksburg.: Harris, *Game of My Life*, p. 25.

34   Hokie fan Trace King decided to propose . . . was also down on one knee.: Madelyn Rosenberg, "Fan's Cheer: 'Rah, Rah, Ree,'" *The Roanoke Times*, Feb. 6, 1997.

34   'Oh, my gosh, he's going to do it.' 'Here?': Rosenberg.

35   "within moments of the final horn, . . . and his elbow gets my tooth.": Doughty and Lazenby, p. 167.

35   "I felt somebody jump on my back," . . . in looking for Beamer's tooth,: Doughty and Lazenby, p. 169.

35   I guess it's good to be remembered for something, . . . the guy who knocked out Frank Beamer's tooth.: Doughty and Lazenby, p. 169.

36   "a real hero for us.": Randy King, "Katie O Is Old-School," *The Roanoke Times*, Feb. 21, 1999.

36   "Her number of charges taken, . . . what Katie O'Connor does for us.": King, "Katie O Is Old-School."

36   "I'm not one of those players . . . try to get some boards.": King, "Katie O Is Old-School."

36   I was brought up with the philosophy . . . as long as we win.": King, "Katie O Is Old-School."

37   Tech athletic director and head football coach Frank . . . the new league -- for fifteen years.: Doughty and Lazenby, p. 71.

37   Tech was excluded because the school's sports program had become too weak for serious consideration.: Doughty and Lazenby, p. 71.

37   By the time Moseley rebuilt the program, . . . they liked their exclusive club the way it was.: Doughty and Lazenby, p. 71.

37   The first thing you know, Tech will win the Atlantic Coast Conference championship.: Doughty and Lazenby, p. 72.

38   Noel had plenty of time and . . . a strike, an easy catch.: Harris, *Game of My Life*, pp. 139-40.

38   "[The pass] came at me . . . debating how to catch the ball.": Harris, *Game of My Life*, p. 140.

38   "That was one play,". . . "the guy who dropped that pass.": Harris, *Game of My Life*, p. 142.

38   Wilford made a promise to . . . best receiver he could be.: Harris, *Game of My Life*, p. 140.

38   I wasn't going to let it beat me. No way.: Harris, *Game of My Life*, p. 140.

39   Some players asserted they were "tougher . . . bragged that nobody could run on them.: Randy King, "Twice as Nice," *The Roanoke Times*, Dec. 7, 2008.

39   "Not one time can I remember anybody . . . "We ran it right down their throats,": King, "Twice as Nice."

39   The Tech offense "lined up, manned up,": King, "Twice as Nice."

40   "one of the hidden stars on a series . . . teammates such as Duke Thorpe, Wayne Robinson, and Dale Solomon,: Harris, *Game of My Life*, p. 204.

40   FSU missed a shot with about five seconds left: Harris, *Game of My Life*, p. 203.

40   Henson chased the ball down . . . "Can you believe that?": Harris, *Game of My Life*, p. 205.

40   It's amazing. Some of the greatest . . . same ones it takes to be a Christian man.: Bettinger, p. 121.

41   Late in the 1966 West Virginia game, . . . "so I didn't do anything.": Schlabach, p. 91.

41   The same player gave a fair-catch signal . . . it was a clean hit.": Schlabach, p. 91.

41   an injury required that Griffith move from guard . . . determined that Griffith's hit had been a cheap shot.: Schlabach, p. 92.

42   Hurd's journey from obscurity . . . a Heisman pose after a field goal.: Randy King, "Holding His Own," *The Roanoke Times*, Dec. 30, 1999.

42   Hurd didn't get a single vote. . . . when you think about it,": King, "Holding His Own."

42   That's a thing I really don't understand.: King, "Holding His Own."

43   The recruiting season had passed . . . and Peer Rogge in Schleswig.: Robby Forbes,

43 "German Give Hokies Kick Start," *The Roanoke Times*, Nov. 1, 2002.
43 gave the Hokies "the boost they needed.": Forbes.
44 Jon Utin grew up in Oxford, England, and . . . to Tech on a Sears & Roebuck scholarship,: Schlabach, p. 107.
44 leading head coach Jerry Claiborne to quip . . . gotten out of a Sears & Roebuck catalog.: Schlabach, pp. 107-8.
44 At Tech, Utin studied, ran track, and played . . . kicked a few times that practice,: Schlabach, p. 108.
44 found a book by legendary kicker Lou Groza . . . what he read there into practice,: Schlabach, p. 109.
44 It was a strange door that brought me . . . like the one that brought me to Tech.: Schlabach, p. 114.
45 "We wanted to get back at them," . . . we wanted to take this game.": Randy King, "Back on Top," *The Roanoke Times*, Dec. 2, 2007.
45 After the Hokies lost to LSU, . . . two-man rotation when Taylor returned.: King, "Back on Top."
45 This was "a redemption thing for Sean, too,": King, "Back on Top."
45 "shows how blessed I've been.": King, "Back on Top."
45 Redemption. That's all we were thinking about this week.: King, "Back on Top."
46 As a sophomore in 1961, he played . . . advised Frank not to quit, and Frank listened.: Schlabach, p. 52.
46 When Frank graduated in June 1963, . . . I'm tough enough to come back for another year.": Schlabach, p. 53.
46 If you quit now, next time the going gets tough, you'll quit again.: Schlabach, p. 52.
47 In the fall of 2001, though, Tugwell . . . improved his ability to hit for power.: Mark Berman, "Putting Time to Good Use," *The Roanoke Times*, May 5, 2003.
47 "You learn your lesson," Tugwell said of the suspension. "It was a blessing in disguise.": Berman, "Putting Time to Good Use."
47 If there's such a thing as a blessing in disguise, that was one.: Berman, "Putting Time to Good Use."
48 the first Tech class to receive football scholarships.: Doughty and Lazenby, p. 36.
48 "fleet back who loved the open field,": "From the Beginning . . . To the Beamer Era," *hokiesports.com*, http://www.hokiesports.com/football/history.html, Oct. 4, 2010.
48 Peake suffered a hip injury against . . . began to beg Gustafson to let him run it.: Doughty and Lazenby, p. 37.
48 The coach relented, and Peake quickly scored. . . . "I told you they wouldn't touch me.": Doughty and Lazenby, p. 38.
49 "an identity crisis.": Colston, *Tales from the Virginia Tech Sideline*, p. 33.
49 as Dooley was hired in 1978, many felt . . . William & Mary, and Richmond.: Colston, *Tales from the Virginia Tech Sideline*, p. 33.
49 "Are we really stepping up, or . . . just to win games against mediocre competition?": Colston, *Tales from the Virginia Tech Sideline*, p. 34.
49 the "tug of war": Colston, *Tales from the Virginia Tech Sideline*, p. 34.
49 offensive coordinator Pat Watson sent equipment . . . all the work gloves he could find.: Colston, *Tales from the Virginia Tech Sideline*, p. 39.
49 After the 54-7 Hokies win, . . . as the reporters stood outside.": Colston, *Tales from the Virginia Tech Sideline*, p. 39.
49 I don't think that we will be returning to the Oyster Bowl.: Colston, *Tales from the Virginia Tech Sideline*, p. 39.
50 Kublina grew up in Latvia . . . Like her other class work -- no problem.: Mark Berman, "Ieva Kublina Was Born in Latvia," *The Roanoke Times*, March 2, 2004.
51 Shayne Graham's last-play, game-winning . . . catch from Vick in the 31-7 win at Virginia.: Randy King, "Virginia Tech's Top 10 Moments of the Season," *The Roanoke Times*, Nov. 26, 1999.
52 He changed motels for his team; . . . were willing to try anything" to get a win.: Randy King, "Hokies Play Their Ace in the Hole," *The Roanoke Times*, Jan. 8, 1995.
52 I don't think we'll ever see this place again.: King, "Hokies Play Their Ace in the Hole."
53 On the day after the 2000 Sugar Bowl, . . . talk about was Michael Vick,": Randy King, "Michael Vick Didn't Expect to Be a Football Hero," *The Roanoke Times*, Aug. 24, 2000.
53 He had "dodged, darted, scrambled and escaped" . . . the same again for Michael Vick.": King, "Michael Vick Didn't Expect."
53 In February, Vick went to Las Vegas . . . surrounded and corralled by fans.: King, "Michael Vick Didn't Expect."
53 Just like that, in the time . . . think about it, it's crazy, man.: King, "Michael Vick Didn't Expect."
54 On a cold night in February 1967,: Schlabach, p. 111.
54 several athletes came in late and gathered . . . with his head just barely above water.: Schlabach, p. 112.
54 They managed to unclog . . . had never seen the floors so clean.: Schlabach, p. 113.
54 Let's open up all the windows and go ice skating.: Schlabach, p. 112.
55 "was a dream squad, the fruit . . . deep in talent at the skill positions.": Doughty and Lazenby, p. 72.
55 The heart and soul of the team was . . . one of the fastest teams in Tech history.": Doughty and Lazenby, p. 73.

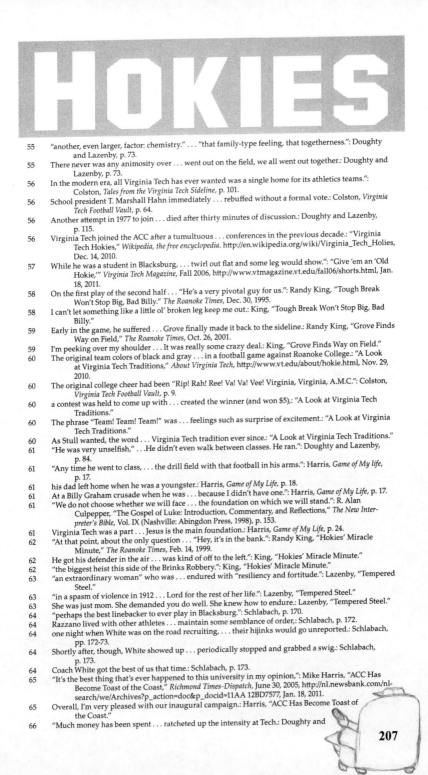

55   "another, even larger, factor: chemistry." . . . "that family-type feeling, that togetherness.": Doughty and Lazenby, p. 73.

55   There never was any animosity over . . . went out on the field, we all went out together.: Doughty and Lazenby, p. 73.

56   In the modern era, all Virginia Tech has ever wanted was a single home for its athletics teams.": Colston, *Tales from the Virginia Tech Sideline*, p. 101.

56   School president T. Marshall Hahn immediately . . . rebuffed without a formal vote.: Colston, *Virginia Tech Football Vault*, p. 64.

56   Another attempt in 1977 to join . . . died after thirty minutes of discussion.: Doughty and Lazenby, p. 115.

56   Virginia Tech joined the ACC after a tumultuous . . . conferences in the previous decade.: "Virginia Tech Hokies," *Wikipedia, the free encyclopedia*. http://en.wikipedia.org/wiki/Virginia_Tech_Holies, Dec. 14, 2010.

57   While he was a student in Blacksburg, . . . twirl out flat and some leg would show.": "Give 'em an 'Old Hokie,'" *Virginia Tech Magazine*, Fall 2006, http://www.vtmagazine.vt.edu/fall06/shorts.html, Jan. 18, 2011.

58   On the first play of the second half . . . "He's a very pivotal guy for us.": Randy King, "Tough Break Won't Stop Big, Bad Billy." *The Roanoke Times*, Dec. 30, 1995.

58   I can't let something like a little ol' broken leg keep me out.: King, "Tough Break Won't Stop Big, Bad Billy."

59   Early in the game, he suffered . . . Grove finally made it back to the sideline.: Randy King, "Grove Finds Way on Field," *The Roanoke Times*, Oct. 26, 2001.

59   I'm peeking over my shoulder . . . It was really some crazy deal.: King, "Grove Finds Way on Field."

60   The original team colors of black and gray . . . in a football game against Roanoke College.: "A Look at Virginia Tech Traditions," *About Virginia Tech*, http://www.vt.edu/about/hokie.html, Nov. 29, 2010.

60   The original college cheer had been "Rip! Rah! Ree! Va! Va! Vee! Virginia, Virginia, A.M.C.": Colston, *Virginia Tech Football Vault*, p. 9.

60   a contest was held to come up with . . . created the winner (and won $5),: "A Look at Virginia Tech Traditions."

60   The phrase "Team! Team! Team!" was . . . feelings such as surprise of excitement.: "A Look at Virginia Tech Traditions."

60   As Stull wanted, the word . . . Virginia Tech tradition ever since.: "A Look at Virginia Tech Traditions."

61   "He was very unselfish," . . . He didn't even walk between classes. He ran.": Doughty and Lazenby, p. 84.

61   "Any time he went to class, . . . the drill field with that football in his arms.": Harris, *Game of My life*, p. 17.

61   his dad left home when he was a youngster.: Harris, *Game of My Life*, p. 18.

61   At a Billy Graham crusade when he was . . . because I didn't have one.": Harris, *Game of My Life*, p. 17.

61   "We do not choose whether we will face . . . the foundation on which we will stand.": R. Alan Culpepper, "The Gospel of Luke: Introduction, Commentary, and Reflections," *The New Interpreter's Bible*, Vol. IX (Nashville: Abingdon Press, 1998), p. 153.

61   Virginia Tech was a part . . . Jesus is the main foundation.: Harris, *Game of My Life*, p. 24.

62   "At that point, about the only question . . . "Hey, it's in the bank.": Randy King, "Hokies' Miracle Minute," *The Roanoke Times*, Feb. 14, 1999.

62   He got his defender in the air . . . was kind of off to the left.": King, "Hokies' Miracle Minute."

62   "the biggest heist this side of the Brinks Robbery.": King, "Hokies' Miracle Minute."

63   "an extraordinary woman" who was . . . endured with "resiliency and fortitude.": Lazenby, "Tempered Steel."

63   "in a spasm of violence in 1912 . . . Lord for the rest of her life.": Lazenby, "Tempered Steel."

63   She was just mom. She demanded you do well. She knew how to endure.: Lazenby, "Tempered Steel."

64   "perhaps the best linebacker to ever play in Blacksburg.": Schlabach, p. 170.

64   Razzano lived with other athletes . . . maintain some semblance of order,: Schlabach, p. 172.

64   one night when White was on the road recruiting, . . . their hijinks would go unreported.: Schlabach, pp. 172-73.

64   Shortly after, though, White showed up . . . periodically stopped and grabbed a swig.: Schlabach, p. 173.

64   Coach White got the best of us that time.: Schlabach, p. 173.

65   "It's the best thing that's ever happened to this university in my opinion,": Mike Harris, "ACC Has Become Toast of the Coast," *Richmond Times-Dispatch*, June 30, 2005, http://nl.newsbank.com/nl-search/we/Archives?p_action=doc&p_docid=11AA 12BD7577, Jan. 18, 2011.

65   Overall, I'm very pleased with our inaugural campaign.: Harris, "ACC Has Become Toast of the Coast."

66   "Much money has been spent . . . ratcheted up the intensity at Tech.: Doughty and

Lazenby, p. 68.

66   "like a war, and we were the survivors.": Colston, *Tales from the Virginia Tech Sideline*, p. 5.

66   By the time Moseley arrived, they had raised almost $10,000,: Doughty and Lazenby, pp. 68-69.

66   the members were eager to meet the new . . . They raised $9,000 more on the spot.: Doughty and Lazenby, p. 69.

67   "He's the type of leader . . . "He's kind of like the preacher on this team.": Randy King, "Inspirational Leader," *The Roanoke Times*, Sept. 26, 2003.

67   The Hokies team of 2003 gathered . . . things in these guys' minds.: King, "Inspirational Leader."

67   As a junior, he was diagnosed . . . a great lesson for a lot of us.": King, "Inspirational Leader."

68   "I was getting ready to say, . . . going to go to in overtime.": Randy King, "Tech Canes Miami," *The Roanoke Times*, Nov. 17, 1996.

68   in the lineup only because the . . . and try to end this thing.": King, "Tech Canes Miami."

68   "I never thought I'd be the one to make the big play,": King, "Tech Canes Miami."

68   Who would have ever imagined Keion Carpenter?: King, "Tech Canes Miami.'

69   "one of the key players in the resurgence of the Virginia Tech program": Harris, *Game of My Life*, p. 77.

69   Jim's older brother had played football . . . Beamer followed his advice.: Harris, *Game of My Life*, p. 78.

69   I don't think you want to listen . . . you'll be sitting up there with them.: Jerry Ratcliffe, "Our League: Lalich Heads West for Next Chapter of College Career," *The Daily Progress*, Sept. 20, 2008, http://www2.dailyprogress.com/sports/cdp-sports-cavinsider/2008/sep/25, Dec. 20, 2010.

70   He played defensive back his first two . . . the process of having quarterbacks come through.": Schlabach, p. 81.

70   "We didn't do much . . . but I never felt like we were in danger" of losing.: Schlabach, p. 84.

70   During the game, coach Jerry Claiborne sent a play . . . Don't let that happen again.": Schlabach, p. 86.

71   it would be 93 years before the Hokies . . . drought stretched across 19 straight losses.:Mark Berman, "Hokies Turn Back Clock 93 Years," *The Roanoke Times*, Feb. 11, 2010.

72   Scales grew up on the streets . . . he lived in the home of a teammate.: Bryan Messerly, "Keep the Faith," *Virginia Tech Magazine*, Fall 1997, http://www.vtmagazine.vt.edu/fall97/sports.html, Dec. 7, 2010.

72   He was heavily recruited by . . . Tech offered him a scholarship.: Messerly.

72   "My whole life has been adversity," . . . "You've got to keep the faith.": Messerly.

72   To me, religion -- faith -- is the only real thing in life.: Bettinger, p. 44.

73   Money was short, the Hokies were on . . . Beamer ever coached a game.: Jack Bogaczyk, "Beamer Tasted Bitter Times Long Before the Sweet," *The Roanoke Times*, Dec. 19, 1999.

73   his future at Tech was anything but secure.: Bogaczyk, "Beamer Tasted Bitter Times."

73   AD Dave Braine delivered an ultimatum . . . have a losing season and we won't.: Bogaczyk, "Beamer Tasted Bitter Times."

73   There were days when I'm sure . . . wondered if [success at Virginia Tech] was possible.: Bogaczyk, "Beamer Tasted Bitter Times."

74   It's a jumping thing.": Mark Berman, "Oh, To Be King for This Day," *The Roanoke Times*, Sept. 25, 2005.

74   King, who is 6-5, teamed with . . . Imhoh stood 5-7.: Berman, "Oh, To Be King for This Day."

74   The Tech offensive guard stepped inside . . . to hop over the guard's leg and block the kick.: Berman, "Oh, To Be King for This Day."

74   "Probably his basketball skills there help him a little bit because it's a jumping thing." Berman, "Oh, To Be King for This Day."

75   the night before the game when . . . what's best for our basketball team.": Randy King, "Too Close for Comfort," *The Roanoke Times*, Feb. 28, 1999.

75   "Without the scrappy Weatherspoon, their unquestioned heart and soul,": King, "Too Close for Comfort."

75   The team "was totally out of sync.": King, "Too Close for Comfort."

75   "At that point we had nothing to lose," . . . we've got to take control.'": King, "Too Close for Comfort."

75   This team won't quit; it never has at anything.: King, "Too Close for Comfort."

76   "I was like fifth-, sixth-, or seventh-team," . . . Two games into the season, Beasley was a starter.: Schlabach, p. 146.

77   "John Moody is singularly responsible for a lot of things that are here at the university,": Albert Raboteau, "Flagpole Plaza at Stadium Named for John Moody," *The Campaign for Virginia Tech*, http://www.campaign.vt.edu/campaign-vt?q=node/331, Dec. 10, 2010.

77   In 1952, he was all set to play football . . . would furnish him a cadet uniform.: Colston, *Tales from the Virginia Tech Sideline*, p. 16.

77   It's amazing how the smallest . . . impacts you for the rest of your life.: Colston, *Tales from the Virginia Tech Sideline*, p. 16.

78   He entered Tech in the fall . . . he was the starting right halfback.: Doughty and Lazenby, p. 25.

78   For all three seasons, though, Carpenter . . . advising his son to do his best when he played.: Doughty and Lazenby, p. 26.

79   History has it that he came in after the . . . to build a top-25 program "out of a closet.": Chuck Altizer,

HOKIES

"The End of 'an Amazing Home-Field Advantage,'" *The Roanoke Times*, Jan. 26, 2010.

79 It was definitely a great home-field advantage.: Altizer.

80 Not a single football scholarship was awarded . . . "but to fight in a gentlemanly way.": Doughty and Lazenby, p. 41.

80 declaring how discouraging it was to see a young man . . . Rather than deal with that attitude,: Doughty and Lazenby, p. 42.

80 Since he had no scholarships to hand out, . . . "smart kids, not really athletes,": Doughty and Lazenby, p. 43.

80 When I look back on it, I don't know how we did it.: Doughty and Lazenby, p. 43.

81 "Akron (1-5) had one chance against Tech (4-2). It was called Zip.": Randy King, "Tech Shows Some Zip," *The Roanoke Times*, Oct. 15, 1995.

81 "I was done after one quarter," . . . we should have hit 120 points.": King, "Tech Shows Some Zip."

81 He started benching his regulars . . . on the Hokies' sideline but the water boys.": King, "Tech Shows Some Zip."

81 "After you see all those points go up, . . . stop taking advantage of young guys.": King, "Tech Shows Some Zip."

81 It's real frustrating. But . . . we're going to need them.: King, "Tech Shows Some Zip."

82 "I've never seen a year like this. Not even close.": Randy King, "Hokies Try to Salvage Difficult Season," *The Roanoke Times*, May 17, 2000.

82 They headed into the Atlantic 10 tournament . . . out there and see what happens.": King, "Hokies Try to Salvage Difficult Season."

82 Despite all we've gone through, we're still not done yet.: King, "Hokies Try to Salvage Difficult Season."

83 I guess I've replayed that Dayton game over in my mind a hundred times.": Mark Berman, "1967: The 1 That Got Away," *The Roanoke Times*, March 20, 2002.

83 the Hokies pretty much had . . . self-destructed going down the wire,": Berman, "1967: The 1 That Got Away."

83 It was "pretty devastating," . . . "We should've won.": Berman, "1967: The 1 That Got Away."

84 He would have snapped up . . . I heard it was a good time,': Randy King, "Coming into His Own," *The Roanoke Times*, Nov. 27, 2009.

84 "I was just happy to be dressing . . . my whole career pretty much.: King, "Coming into His Own."

84 "despicable, vile, unprincipled, scoundrels.": MacArthur, p. 152.

84 It feels good to have the kind of success I have had. I never really expected this. It's really cool.: King, "Coming into His Own."

85 "maybe the greatest stand in Virginia Tech history. I guarantee you it was the stand of the century.": Harris, *Game of My Life*, p. 58.

85 That was the greatest display of guts and sportsmanship I've ever been associated with.: Harris, *Game of My Life*, p. 58.

86 He gave up basketball only because . . . left him struggling to keep up academically.: Schlabach, p. 18.

86 Virginia Tech had the early lead in its . . . Tech had no such rule.: Schlabach, p. 18.

86 I can't adequately describe to you the love that permeates a good football team.: Ken Rappaport, *The Nittany Lions: Penn State Football* (Tomball, TX: The Strode Publishers, 1987), p. 296.

87 Her parents drove seventeen hours from Ashland, Penn., to Gainesville, Fla., for the game.: Randy King, "Wetzel Pays Back Parents for Long Trip," *The Roanoke Times*, March 15, 1998.

87 "I went out there and I was just . . . of feeling I've never really felt in me.": King, "Wetzel Pays Back Parents for Long Trip."

87 I knew I had to do something good for [my parents].: King, "Wetzel Pays Back Parents for Long Trip."

88 It was the first, the last, and the only time. . . one-fourth of their allotted tickets.: Doug Doughty, "Cold Down to Your Tights," *The Roanoke Times*, Nov. 29, 2002.

88 All I remember was it was bitterly cold.: Doughty, "Cold Down to Your Tights."

89 Offensive coordinator Rickey Bustle sent down a play . . . what the heck is he doing now?'": Jack Bogaczyk, "Everything He Touches Turns to Gold," *The Raleigh Times*, Dec. 11, 1999.

90 "put fire in the eyes of the defeated and fear in the hearts of the weak.": Doughty and Lazenby, p. 67.

90 After losing their coach, Jimmy Kitts, . . . "overachieving smart kids who wanted to play.": Doughty and Lazenby, p. 55.

90 Most of the veterans had had more than . . . "They just didn't get the players anymore,": Doughty and Lazenby, p. 62.

90 After one four-hour interview, the council . . . lucrative contract ever for a Tech coach.: Doughty and Lazenby, p. 68.

90 he boldly announced Tech would have a winning season within five years.: Doughty and Lazenby, p. 69.

90 Frank Moseley came to Blacksburg . . .winless misery to the age of big-time athletics.: Doughty and Lazenby, p. 67.

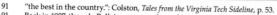

91   "the best in the country.": Colston, *Tales from the Virginia Tech Sideline*, p. 53.

91   Back in 1987, though, Ballein was a . . . showed it to assistant coach Billy Hite,: Colston, *Tales from the Virginia Tech Sideline*, p. 51.

91   who was not at all impressed. . . . a chance as a Tech graduate assistant.: Colston, *Tales from the Virginia Tech Sideline*, p. 51.

91   I'm a pretty good judge of character, but I was wrong that time.: Colston, *Tales from the Virginia Tech Sideline*, p. 51.

92   who had earned a scholarship in 2008 primarily because of his excellence on special teams.: Randy King, "Tech's Reidy Sudden Celebrity," *The Roanoke Times*, Sept. 30, 2009.

92   "a total rear-end kicking in all phases of the game.": Randy King, "Hokies Wet 'n' Wild," *The Roanoke Times*, Sept. 27, 2009.

92   Reidy hurried toward the ball . . . never thought I would score in college,": King, "Tech's Reidy Sudden Celebrity."

93   During the evening of Jan, 3, 1974, Hokie head coach . . . left town the next morning.: Doughty and Lazenby, p. 110.

93   He didn't have a quarterback to run . . . all eleven games unless you break a leg.": Doughty and Lazenby, p. 110.

94   Ollendick cleared the bar at . . . broke out in laughter and told her the truth,: Randy King, "Tech High-Jumper Raises the Bar," *The Roanoke Times*, March 28, 1998.

94   An agonizing wait. A horrible wait.: King, "Tech High-Jumper Raises the Bar."

95   he played opposite a Duke guard . . . what do you think I ought to be?": Colston, *Tales from the Virginia Tech Sideline*, p. 14.

95   "I realized that I had lost my desire . . . McCubbin didn't get the part.: Colston, *Tales from the Virginia Tech Sideline*, p. 14.

96   He got the ball seven straight times on Tech's first possession.: Harris, *Game of My Life*, p. 168.

96   "It would have been nice to take it to the house,": Harris, *Game of My Life*, p. 168.

96   and received some ribbing from teammates,: Harris, *Game of My Life*, p. 170.

96   Imoh even called Jones and . . . credited to another back.: Harris, *Game of My Life*, p. 170.

96   Officials from Tech's sports information . . . made the change in the official game records.: Harris, *Game of My Life*, p. 172.

97   Students camped out to get tickets, . . . an electric atmosphere from start to finish.": Harris, *Game of My Life*, p. 217.

97   With a little more than three minutes . . . was pretty much anywhere in the arena.": Harris, *Game of My Life*, p. 215.

97   The Hokies held their usual postgame team meeting . . . out there that long after the game,": Harris, *Game of My Life*, p. 217.

97   The place didn't go berserk. It just stayed that way.: Harris, *Game of My Life*, p. 215.

98   "tough son of a gun" . . . a 5 feet, 10 inch cornerback shouldn't do.": Harris, *Game of My Life*, p. 32.

98   he had a fondness for players . . . lot faster than I was.": Harris, *Game of My Life*, pp. 37, 39.

98   he had "that football sense" that enabled him "to get myself to the right place at the right time.": *Game of My Life*, Harris, p. 33.

98   That evening he had a blind date with a young woman named Cheryl Oakley.: Harris, *Game of My Life*, p. 37.

99   Most of the skepticism surrounding Tech's . . . didn't think we could beat Virginia.": Doughty and Lazenby, p. 127.

99   I've never seen a team that wanted to win a game so much.: Doughty and Lazenby, p. 127.

100   Oates became the first person in Virginia Tech . . . going to be longer than 14 months.": Mark Berman, "Ceremony Adds to Tech Great Oates' Many Thrills," *The Roanoke Times*, May 5, 2002.

100   Oates said he always felt that . . . go back to that football training.": Berman, "Ceremony Adds to Tech Great Oates' Many Thrills."

100   "When you look at it, it's a blessing," . . . mattered the most to him -- his family.: "Johnny Oates Loses Battle to Brain Cancer," *USATODAY.com*, Dec. 26, 2004, http://www.usatoday.com/sports/baseball/2004-12-24-oates-obit_x.html, Jan. 17, 2011.

100   No, no, no, no, no. . . . that I feel so at peace.: Berman, "Ceremony Adds to Tech Great Oates' Many Thrills."

HOKIES

BIBLIOGRAPHY

Altizer, Chuck. "The End of 'an Amazing Home-field Advantage.'" *The Roanoke Times*. 26 Jan. 2010.

Berman, Mark. "1967: The 1 That Got Away: Tech Became 1st Team from State of Virginia to Reach NCAA's Final 8, But Fell to Dayton in OT." *The Roanoke Times*. 20 March 2002.

---. "Angela Tincher Pitches No-Hitter." *The Roanoke Times*. 28 March 2008.

---. "Ceremony Adds to Tech Great Oates' Many Thrills: Former Big-League Player, Manager 1st to Have Hokies Baseball Jersey Retired." *The Roanoke Times*. 5 May 2002.

---. "Greek Thrower Gains Lofty Status: Jullien Competes for Hokies at NCAA Championships." *The Roanoke Times*. 9 June 2003.

---. "His 9 Innings of Fame: 'I'm Never Usually the Highlight of the Team.'" *The Roanoke Times*. 26 April 2002.

---. "Hokies Break Through." *The Roanoke Times*. 19 April 2010.

---. "Hokies Get Last Gasp." *The Roanoke Times*. 29 Jan. 2010.

---. "Hokies Turn Back Clock 93 Years." *The Roanoke Times*. 11 Feb. 2010.

---. "Ieva Kublina Was Born in Latvia, But Her Basketball Skills Are Made in America." *The Roanoke Times*. 2 March 2004.

---. "Oh, To Be King for This Day." *The Roanoke Times*. 25 Sept. 2005.

---. "Putting Time to Good Use." *The Roanoke Times*. 5 May 2003.

Bettinger, Jim & Julie S. *The Book of Bowden*. Nashville: TowleHouse Publishing, 2001.

Bogaczyk, Jack. "Everything He Touches Turns to Gold." *The Roanoke Times*. 11 Dec. 1999.

---. "Beamer Tasted Bitter Times Long Before the Sweet." *The Roanoke Times*. 19 Dec. 1999.

Colston, Chris. *Tales from the Virginia Tech Sideline*. Champaign, IL: Sports Publishing L.L.C., 2007

---. *Virginia Tech Football Vault: The History of the Hokies*. Atlanta: Whitman Publishing, LLC, 2009.

Culpepper, R. Alan. "The Gospel of Luke: Introduction, Commentary, and Reflections." *The New Interpreter's Bible*. Vol. IX. Nashville: Abingdon Press, 1998. 1-490.

Doughty, Doug. "Cold Down to Your Tights." *The Roanoke Times*. 29 Nov. 2002.

Doughty, Doug and Roland Lazenby. *'Hoos 'N' Hokies The Rivalry: 100 Years of Virginia/Virginia Tech Football*. Dallas: Taylor Publishing Company, 1995.

Emerick, Thomas. "Larson Overcomes Setbacks to Enjoy Success." CollegiateTimes.com. 4 April 2008. http://www.collegiatetimes.com/stories/11099.

"Filling the Need." Virginia Tech Magazine. Spring 2008. http://www.vtmagazine.edu/spring08/sports.html.

Forbes, Robby. "Germans Give Hokies Kick Start: A Quick Fix on the Pitch." *The Roanoke Times*. 1 Nov. 2002.

"From Gobbler to HokieBird." *About Virginia Tech*. http://www.vt.edu/about/hokie.html.

"From the Beginning . . . To the Beamer Era." hokiesports.com. http://www.hokiesports.com/football/history.html.

"Give 'em an 'Old Hokie.'" Virginia Tech Magazine. Fall 2006. http://www.vtmagazine.vt.edu/fall06/shorts.html.

Harris, Mike. "ACC Has Become Toast of the Coast: Tech Thrived as Rookie in Confernce." *Richmond Times-Dispatch*. 30 June 2005. http://nl.newsbank.com/nl-search/we/Archives?p_action=doc&p_docid=11AA12BD7577.

---. *Game of My Life: Virginia Tech*. Champaign, IL: Sports Publishing L.L.C., 2006.

Hass, Bill. "Bill Hass on the ACC: Just Call Him Macho Harris and Watch Him Change a Game." TheACC.com. 3 Dec. 2008. http://www.theacc.com/sports/m-footbal/spec-rel/120308aaa.html.

"Johnny Oates Loses Battle to Brain Cancer." USATODAY.com. 26 Dec. 2004. http://www.usatoday.com/sports/baseball/2004-12-24-oates-obit_x.html.

King, Randy. "Back on Top." *The Roanoke Times*. 2 Dec. 2007.

---. "Coming into His Own." *The Roanoke Times*, 27 Nov. 2009.

---. "Grove Finds Way on Field: Sophomore a Mainstay on Tech Offensive Line." *The Roanoke Times*. 26 Oct. 2001.

---. "Hokies' Miracle Minute." *The Roanoke Times*. 14 Feb. 1999.

---. "Hokies Play Their Ace in the Hole to End Eagles' Hex." *The Roanoke Times*. 8 Jan. 1995.

---. "Hokies Shuck Huskers' Upset Bid." *The Roanoke Times*. 20 Sept. 2009.

---. "Hokies Try to Salvage Difficult Season." *The Roanoke Times*. 17 May 2000.

---. "Hokies Wet 'n' Wild." *The Roanoke Times*. 27 Sept. 2009.

---. "Holding His Own." *The Roanoke Times*. 30 Dec. 1999.

---. "Inspirational Leader: Crawford Serves Hokies in Chapel and on Defense." *The Roanoke Times*. 26 Sept. 2003.

---. "Katie O Is Old-School." The Roanoke Times. 21 Feb. 1999.

---. "Making His Dad Proud." *The Roanoke Times.* 16 Oct. 2009.

---. "Michael Vick Didn't Expect to Be a Football Hero, But His Performance in the Sugar Bowl Made It Happen." *The Roanoke Times.* 24 Aug. 2000.

---. "No Longer a String Bean." *The Roanoke Times.* 25 Aug. 2000.

---. "Quite the Surprise." *The Roanoke Times.* 21 Sept. 2008.

---. "Tech Canes Miami: Carpenter Nails Down Win with Interception Return." *The Roanoke Times.* 17 Nov. 1996.

---. "Tech High Jumper Raises the Bar: Ollendick Is Hokies' First All-American Since 1987." *The Roanoke Times.* 28 March 1998.

---. "Tech Shows Some Zip: The Hokies Get What They Need -- an Offensive Explosion -- in a 77-27 Victory over the Akron Zips." *The Roanoke Times.* 15 Oct. 1995.

---. "Tech's Reidy Sudden Celebrity." *The Roanoke Times.* 30 Sept. 2009.

---. "Too Close for Comfort." *The Roanoke Times.* 28 Feb. 1999.

---. "Tough Break Won't Stop Big, Bad Billy." *The Roanoke Times.* 30 Dec. 1995.

---. "Turning on the Juice." *The Roanoke Times.* 17 Oct. 1999.

---. "Twice as Nice." *The Roanoke Times,* 7 Dec. 2008.

---. "Uncalled Trickery a Treat for Hokies." *The Roanoke Times.* 30 Sept. 2001.

---. "Virginia Tech's Top 10 Moments of the Season." *The Roanoke Times.* 26 Nov. 1999.

---. "Wetzel Pays Back Parents for Long Trip: Father and Mother Drive 17 Hours to See Daughter Play.": *The Roanoke Times.* 15 March 1998.

Klopman, Michael. "Greg Nosal, Virginia Tech Left Guard, Loses FINGER Tip During Game." *The Huffington Post.* 11 Oct. 2010. http://www.huffingtonpost.com/2010/10/11/greg-nosal-loses-finger_n_758524.html.

Lazenby, Roland. "Tempered Steel: How Frank Beamer Got That Way.": *The Roanoker.* 15 Dec. 2010. http://theroanoker.com/interests/teampered-steel-how-frank-beamer-got-that-way-2010.

"A Look at Virginia Tech Traditions." *About Virginia Tech.* http://www.vt.edu/about/hokie.html.

MacArthur, John. *Twelve Ordinary Men.* Nashville: W Publishing Group, 2002.

McFarling, Aaron. "Come-from-Behind Win Leaves Hokies Giddy." *The Roanoke Times.* 21 Sept. 2008.

Messerly, Bryan. "Keep the Faith." *Virginia Tech Magazine.* Fall 1997. http://www.vtmagazine.vt.edu/fall97/sports.html.

Pieper, Lindsay. "Va. Tech Title-Holder Trades Concertos for Championships." *CBSSports.com.* 2 May 2006. http://www.cstv.com/sports/c-track/u-wire/050206aad.html.

Raboteau, Albert. "Flagpole Plaza at Stadium Named for John Moody." *The Campaign for Virginia Tech.* http://www.campaign.vt.edu/campaign-vt?q=node/331.

Rappaport, Ken. *The Nittany Lions: Penn State Football.* Tomball TX: The Strode Publishers, 1987.

Ratcliffe, Jerry. "Our League: Lalich Heads West for Next Chapter of College Career." *The Daily Progress.* 25 Sept. 2008. http://www2.dailyprogress.com/sports/cdp-sports-cavinsider/2008/sep/25.

Reisinger, Tyler, "Virginia Tech Lineman Severs Pinkie Finger, Stays in Game, Shames You with Toughness." *Sportsgrid.com.* 12 Oct. 2010. http://www.sportsgrid.com/ncaa-football/virginia-tech-lineman-severs-pinkie-finger.

Robertson, Jimmy. "Tennis Team Hopes to Ace Competition with Its Unique Freshman Star." *Virginia Tech Magazine.* Spring 2005. http://www.vtmagazine.vt.edu/spring05/sports.html.

Rosenberg, Madelyn. "Fan's Cheer: 'Rah, Rah, Ree, Will You Marry Me?'" *The Roanoke Times.* 6 Feb. 1997.

Schlabach, Mark. *What It Means to Be a Hokie: Frank Beamer and Virginia Tech's Greatest Players.* Chicago: Triumph Books, 2006.

Sumner, Jim. "Looking Back: Virginia Tech's Road to the 1973 NIT Title." *TheACC.com.* 18 Feb. 2009. http://www.theacc.com/sports/m-baskbl/spec-rel/021809aaa.html.

"Tennis Phenom J.J. Larson Does Things Just Like Everyone Else Despite a Birth Defect, Sometimes Better." *redOrbit.com.* 10 June 2005. http://www.redorbit.com/news/health/155160.

"Virginia Tech Hokies." *Wikipedia, the free encyclopedia.* http://en.wikipedia.org/wiki/Virginia_Tech Hokies.

INDEX OF NAMES
(LAST NAME, FIRST NAME, DEVOTION DAY NUMBER)

213

214